The Struggle for the Pontic Steppe

Russo-Ottoman Wars 1768-1792

Dave Watson

Balkan Military History

The Struggle for the Pontic Steppe

Russo-Ottoman Wars 1768-1792

Dave Watson

Balkan Military History

Copyright © Dave Watson 2025

The right of Dave Watson to be identified as the author of this book has been asserted by him in accordance with the Copyright, Designs and Patents Act of 1988.

All rights reserved. No part of this book may be reproduced or transmitted in any form or by any means, electronic or mechanical, including photocopying, recording, or by any information storage and retrieval system, without the prior permission of the author in writing.

Pictures are in the public domain or the author's collection unless stated otherwise. Every reasonable effort has been made to trace copyright holders and to obtain their permission for the use of copyrighted material. The author and publisher apologise for any errors and omissions in this work, and would be grateful if notified of any corrections that should be incorporated in future editions of this book.

Balkan Military History

www.balkanhistory.org

ISBN: 978-1-9193086-0-9 (paperback)

ISBN: 978-1-9193086-1-6 (ebook)

Contents

1. Introduction — 1
2. Chronology — 5
3. Europe in the 18th Century — 7
4. The Russian Empire — 11
5. The Ottoman Empire — 23
6. The Russian Army — 32
7. The Ottoman Army — 52
8. The Balkans and Crimea, 1768–74 — 67
9. War in the Caucasus — 91
10. Naval Warfare and the Mediterranean — 97
11. Peace and the Interregnum — 109
12. War Resumes, 1787–92 — 124
13. Conclusion — 141
14. Annex: Wargaming the Conflict — 144
15. Bibliography — 156
16. About the Author — 160

Chapter One

Introduction

This book examines the conflict between the Russian and Ottoman empires for control of the Pontic Steppe region during the second half of the 18th century. The Pontic Steppe stretches from the northern shores of the Black Sea to the northern area around the Caspian Sea. In modern national terms, this region spans from northeastern Bulgaria and southeastern Romania through Moldova, Ukraine, and southern Russia to the North Caucasus. In antiquity, tribes of nomadic horsemen, including the Scythians and Sarmatians, used the steppe, probably domesticating horses for the first time, and many migrated into Europe. A recent study suggests that it was the homeland of the speakers of the Proto-Indo-European language, now spoken by almost half the world's population[1].

The Russo-Ottoman Wars of 1768–74 and 1787–92 were fought for control of this region, occasionally spilling over to the southern Caucasus, the wider Balkans, and the Mediterranean. They were two of twelve wars between 1568 and 1918 that marked the struggle for dominance between the Russian and Ottoman empires. This conflict had far-reaching consequences for both empires and the broader European geopolitical landscape.

The conflict was rooted in longstanding tensions between the Russian and Ottoman Empires, and was primarily driven by Catherine the Great's expansionist policies, support for Orthodox Christians in Ottoman territories, and ambitions to secure access to warm-water ports. The Ottoman Empire sought to maintain its territorial integrity and counter Russian encroachments.

The Seat of War on the Pontic Steppe

In 1768, the immediate cause of the war was Poland, where Russian forces clashed with pro-Ottoman factions during the internal turmoil of the Polish-Lithuanian Commonwealth. The Ottomans, alarmed by Russian interference in their sphere of influence, declared war on Russia on 6 October 1768. In January 1769, a large Ottoman-Tatar army led by Crimean Khan Qirim Giray invaded central Ukraine, ravaging settlements and enslaving people.

The primary front was in the Balkans and eastwards into modern-day Ukraine and Crimea when Russian forces invaded Ottoman territories, securing key victories and gaining support from local Christian populations. The Russian navy moved from the Baltic to the Mediterranean and achieved several decisive victories, including the Battle of Chesme (Chesma) in 1770, which crippled the Ottoman fleet. The Russians also pushed into the Caucasus region, further weakening Ottoman control, and encouraged revolts in Greece and the Levant.

The war ended with the Treaty of Küçük Kaynarca (Kuchuk-Kainarji) in 1774, in which Russia gained territory, including access to the Black Sea coast. The Crimean Khanate was declared independent, effectively placing it under Russian influence. Russia also claimed it was granted the right to protect Orthodox Christians within the Ottoman Empire, thereby bolstering its influence in the Balkans. Russian ships were able to navigate freely in the Black Sea and pass through the Bosporus and Dardanelles.

The Treaty of Küçük Kaynarca was merely a respite. In 1787, Russia annexed Crimea, and the war resumed. This time, Austria was allied with Russia, and this led to a broader conflict in the Balkans. Britain, formerly allied to Russia, and the French both encouraged the Ottomans to resist. The Ottomans attacked the Russian fortresses in southern Ukraine, but were defeated by the Russian General Alexander Suvorov. He went on to invade Moldavia, capturing key fortresses and defeating the Ottomans at the battles of Focşani and Rymnik in modern Romania. The Austrians cooperated in this campaign, although with mixed success. Suvorov captured Izmail at the entrance of the Danube in December 1790, which led to a further victory at Machin in July 1791.

Wider European events, including Prussian hostility and the French Revolution, encouraged Russia to agree to a truce. The Treaty of Jassy (Iaşi) was signed on 9 January 1792, recognising Russia's 1783 annexation of the Crimean Khanate. Odessa and Ochakov were also ceded to Russia, and the Dniester was made the Russian frontier in Europe. The Russian Asiatic frontier along the Kuban River remained unchanged. This is where our story ends. War broke out again in 1806, with fighting over similar ground along the Danube, but this conflict became part of the wider Napoleonic Wars.

The conflict marked a turning point in the decline of the Ottoman Empire and the rise of Russia as a major European power. It strengthened Russia's geopolitical position and set the stage for future conflicts in the region. It would take two further wars to establish Russian control of the entire north coast of the Black Sea.

We will cover all the theatres of the war in a book aimed at the generalist historical reader who wants to learn more about a conflict that is unfamiliar to Western audiences and has particular relevance today. If you are looking for an academic study, we highly recommend Brian Davies' book, *The Russo-Turkish War, 1768–1774*, and anything by Virginia Aksan on the Ottomans. Simon Sebag Montefiore's authoritative *The Life of Potemkin* is also an excellent read. The bibliography at the end of this book provides further sources for those who wish to explore the subject in more detail. We will examine the armies involved in some detail, and in the annex, offer suggestions for recreating the battles on the tabletop, including scenarios to help wargamers get started in this fascinating and relatively overlooked period.

Most historians tend to refer to these conflicts as the Russo-Turkish Wars, as this term has become the standard. However, the Ottoman Empire during this period was neither geographically nor ethnically confined to Turkey, so we refer, admittedly pedantically, to the Ottomans. Place names have changed many times over the years, and we use recognisable names with other versions in brackets. The exception is Constantinople, which didn't officially become Istanbul until 1923. Ottoman ranks, systems, and troop types were referred to by a variety of names, which can be confusing even to those who have spent a lifetime studying the records. Dates can also be confusing, as Russia used the Old Style Julian Calendar (OS) until 1918, and sources often use both, without clarification. The Julian Calendar (NS) was eleven days behind the Gregorian dates during this period. Some Ottoman texts use the Islamic calendar, which differs significantly. This is not an academic study, so referencing is used to guide readers who seek more detailed information than space allows in this book.

This conflict resonates with the Russian invasion of Ukraine today. It also means that the historiography can be contested and linked to issues of identity and nationalism. In Russia, the narrative of southward expansion has evolved over the centuries to the point where the current regime claims that Russia was never a colonial power. These wars did not initiate or conclude Russian colonisation; as the Imperial Russian historian Vasily Klyuchevsky stated, it was 'the basic fact of Russian history.' Russian expansionism in the Pontic Steppe was not the typical overseas colonisation practised by Western European powers, and involved displacing another empire. However, Webster's Encyclopedic Dictionary defines colonialism as 'the system or policy of a nation seeking to extend or retain its authority over other people or territories,' which applies to Russia in the 18th century, when it expanded into regions that were not ethnically Russian until settlers were imposed. As Khodarkovsky notes, 'Russia was no less a colonial empire than any of the other Western European powers.' Russia's colonial empire was also built by subjecting indigenous societies; the only difference was that these societies were on its borders rather than overseas.

Chapter Two

Chronology

Date*   **Event**

30 October 1757: Sultan Mustafa III ascends the Ottoman throne.
22 September 1762: Catherine II (the Great) is crowned Empress of Russia.
29 February 1768: Creation of the Bar Confederation in Poland.
7 October 1769: Russian First Army (Rumiantsev) captures Jassy (Iași).
17 November 1769: Russians capture Bucharest.
Jan/Feb 1770: Russian attacks on Ibrail and Giurgiu repulsed.
7 July 1770: Battle of Larga. Rumiantsev defeats (mostly) the Tatar army.
1 August 1770: Battle of Kagul (Cahul). Rumiantsev defeats the Ottoman field army.
16 September 1770: Panin's Russian Second Army captures Bender.
July/Sept 1770: Repnin captures Ottoman fortresses at Ismail, Kilia and Akkerman.
17 February 1770: First squadron of the Russian fleet arrives off the Mani coast, Greece. The Greek revolt breaks out, but is crushed by June.
19 February 1770: The First Partition of Poland is signed in Vienna.
20 April 1770: Battle of Aspindza. King Heraclius of Georgia defeats the Ottomans.
5–7 July 1770: Battle of Chesma. The Ottoman fleet is destroyed.
6 August 1770: Russians (Totleben) help King Solomon I of Imereti recover his capital, Kutaisi, but fail to capture Poti.
9 November 1770: The Ottomans abandon Ibrail.
17 February 1771: Russians (Olits) capture Giurgiu, but are recaptured on 29 May.
June 1771: Dolgorukov invades Crimea, captures Kaffa, and khan abdicates.
June 1771: Ali Bey, the Mamluk governor of Egypt, captures Damascus.
7 August 1771: The Russians (Essen) attack on Giurgiu is repulsed.
20 October 1771: The Ottoman (Ahmet Pasha) attack on Bucharest is defeated. Giurgiu falls.

30 May 1772: The armistice is agreed upon until March 1773.
June 1772: Russian fleet (Orlov) attacks Beirut in support of the Levant revolt.
21 May 1773: Battle of Turtukai. Suvorov's first victory against the Ottomans.
June 1773: Rumiantsev crosses the Danube but fails to capture Silistra and withdraws. War of outposts for the rest of the year.
July 1773: Russian fleet returns to Beirut and occupies the city until January 1774.
September 1773: The Pugachev rebellion starts. Continues until 1775.
21 January 1774: Sultan Mustafa III dies. Sultan Abdul Hamid I takes the throne.
April 1774: Russian First Army crosses the Danube.
20 June 1774: Battle of Kozludza. Suvrov and Kamensky defeat the Ottoman forces of Abdul-Rezak Pasha.
21 July 1774: The Treaty of Küçük Kaynarca ends the war.
May–June 1781: Austro-Russian Alliance.
8 April 1783: Russian annexation of Crimea.
24 July 1783: The Treaty of Georgievsk brings eastern Georgia under Russian protection.
June 1785: Imam Mansur's rebellion in Chechnya. The Russians are defeated at the Battle of Aldy. Rebellion defeated at Battle of Tatartüp, November 1785.
19 August 1787: Russia declares war on the Ottoman Empire.
September 1787: The first of three Russian attempts to capture the Ottoman fortress of Anapa in Circassia. Third succeeds in January 1991.
12 October 1787: Battle of Kinburn. Suvorov defeats the Ottoman amphibious landing.
May–Dec. 1788: Siege of Ochakov. Russians capture fortress on the Dneiper estuary.
June 1788: The Ottoman fleet is defeated by Nassau and Jones off Ochakov.
14 July 1788: Battle of Fidonisi. The Ottoman fleet withdraws to Ochakov.
7 April 1789: Sultan Abdul Hamid I dies. Sultan Selim III takes the throne.
1 August 1789: Battle of Focşani. Russo-Austrian army defeats Yusuf Pasha.
22 September 1789: Battle of Rymnik. Suvorov rescues the Austrians and defeats another Ottoman army.
8–9 September 1790: Battle of Tendra. Ushakov defeats an Ottoman fleet.
December 1790: Siege of Ismail. Suvorov storms the Danube fortress.
8–9 July 1791: Battle of Măcin. Kutuzov outflanks Ottoman forces.
4 August 1791: Treaty of Sistova. Austrians reach a separate peace with the Ottomans.
16 October 1791: Potemkin dies.
9 January 1792: The Treaty of Jassy (Iaşi) ends the war.
17 November 1796: Catherine II (the Great) dies.
   *All dates are in the New Style.

Chapter Three

Europe in the 18th Century

The 18th century was a pivotal period in European history, marked by significant intellectual, political, social, and economic developments. It was an era of enlightenment and the reshaping of global influence through colonial expansion, often referred to as the Age of Enlightenment. Philosophers such as Voltaire, Montesquieu, Rousseau, and Locke advocated for reason, liberty, and the scientific method. Key ideas included the separation of powers, individual rights, religious tolerance, and scepticism towards absolute monarchy.

These ideas greatly influenced political and social movements, including the American and French revolutions. However, the first half of the century was still dominated by absolute monarchies. France under Louis XIV (until 1715) and Louis XV exemplified centralised royal authority. Russia, under rulers like Peter the Great and Catherine the Great, expanded and modernised its empire. The Austrian Habsburgs maintained significant influence in Central and Eastern Europe, while Prussia, under leaders such as Frederick the Great, became a powerful military and cultural force. The exception to absolutism was Britain. Following the Glorious Revolution of 1688, Britain established a constitutional monarchy, striking a balance between the monarchy and Parliament. The Ottomans appeared to be absolute, but in practice, the vastness of the Empire meant that local leaders gained increasing power.

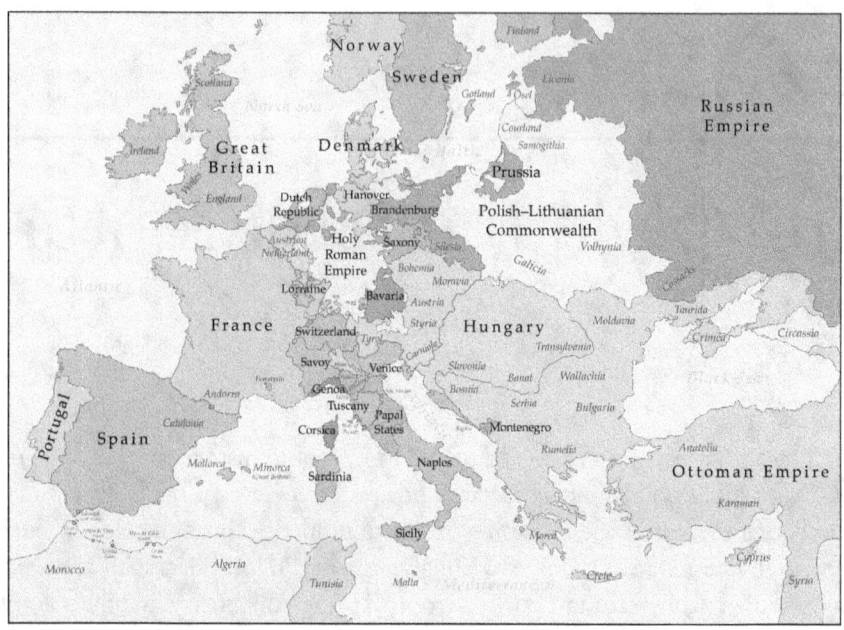

Europe 1748–1766 (P. S. Burton, CC BY 3.0)

This was a period of economic and social development. The agricultural revolution introduced innovations such as crop rotation, selective breeding, and new tools, which increased food production and supported population growth. The 18th century also marked the beginning of the Industrial Revolution, particularly in Britain. European nations, especially Britain, France, and Spain, expanded their overseas empires, boosting global trade but also resulting in exploitation and slavery. The century produced some of the greatest composers, including Bach, Handel, Haydn, and Mozart. Advances in science, led by figures such as Newton and Linnaeus, and literary works by authors like Voltaire and Goethe, significantly shaped European culture.

The period from 1700 to 1768 in Western Europe was characterised by major military conflicts driven by dynastic struggles, territorial ambitions, and the balance of power among European nations. The War of the Spanish Succession (1701–1714) was fought over the Spanish throne, pitting France and Spain against Great Britain, the Dutch Republic, Austria, and other European powers. It concluded with the Treaty of Utrecht, which altered European borders and colonial holdings. As a result, Spain lost territories in Italy; later, it attempted to regain them during the War of the Quadruple Alliance (1718–1720). Britain and Spain clashed again in the Americas during the wonderfully named War of Jenkins' Ear (1739–1748).

The War of the Austrian Succession (1740–1748) was primarily fought over succession disputes following the death of Charles VI and the Pragmatic Sanction, which designated Maria Theresa as the heir. Austria, Britain, and the Dutch Republic fought alongside other nations against Prussia, France, Spain, and Bavaria. The Treaty of Aix-la-Chapelle (1748) ended the war, with Austria retaining the Habsburg throne, but Prussia gained Silesia. This was followed by the Seven Years' War (1756–1763), often referred to as the first global war, as the conflict was fought in India, America, and other colonial possessions, as well as in Europe. Britain, Prussia, and Portugal fought against France, Austria, Russia, Spain, and Sweden. Britain emerged as the dominant colonial power, gaining territories in North America and India, while Prussia maintained its control over Silesia.

In Eastern and Northern Europe, the century began with the Great Northern War (1700–1721), during which a coalition of Russia, Denmark-Norway, Poland-Lithuania, Saxony, and Prussia sought to challenge Swedish dominance in the Baltic. Russia emerged as a significant European power, seizing substantial Baltic territories, while Sweden's influence waned. However, Peter the Great nearly faced disaster when he was defeated by the Ottomans while pursuing the Swedish king after his notable victory at Poltava in 1709. A favourable treaty (likely obtained through bribery) saved Peter from imprisonment, which might have significantly altered the course of Russian history. The War of the Polish Succession (1733–1738) was fought over a contested succession to the Polish throne following the death of Augustus II. France, Spain, and Sardinia opposed Austria, Russia, and other countries that supported Augustus III as king of Poland.

The Austrians and the Ottomans fought two major wars. In the Austro-Turkish War (1716–1718), the Ottomans were defeated by Austria under Prince Eugene of Savoy. The Treaty of Passarowitz (1718) concluded the war, with Austria gaining control of northern Serbia, parts of Bosnia, and the Banat region. Austria came to Russia's support in 1737 but was defeated, ceding northern Serbia and parts of Wallachia back to the Ottomans. Russia's ambitions to expand into Ottoman territories in the Black Sea region resulted in modest gains, with the Ottomans ceding Azov to Russia. Despite Austria's defeat by the Ottomans, many in Russia viewed an alliance with Austria as a vital constraint on the Ottomans. The alliance was confirmed in secret articles in 1746, with both sides agreeing to support each other if war broke out with the Ottomans, excluding Italy and Russia's Asiatic domains. However, the Austrians did not consider themselves bound by this in 1768. The Ottomans also faced wars on two fronts with a series of clashes with the Persians between 1722 and 1746, mainly over territorial disputes in the Caucasus and Iraq. The Treaty of Kerden (1746) restored pre-war borders.

It is often argued that the 18th century marked the beginning of the Ottoman Empire's decline as European powers expanded their influence at the expense of

Ottoman territories. However, before the 1768 war, the Ottomans had held their own against Russia and Austria. They benefited from a period of peace, as they avoided any significant entanglement in the major European wars. It was clear that Russia, rather than Austria, would be the primary threat to the Ottomans as Catherine the Great's (1762–1796) expansionist polices focused on Ottoman territories. The Ottoman Empire was beginning to show the internal stresses that would become more apparent in the following century. It wasn't yet 'the sick man of Europe', yet discontent with rising taxes and ineffective government was leading to a breakdown of the central government. Conservative religious and military forces resisted reform. As Barbara Jelavich concludes, 'Unfortunately for those who saw the necessity of radical reform, the Ottoman Empire had enjoyed a glorious past history. It was difficult for many to believe that there was anything fundamentally wrong with the basic principles on which their government rested.'[1]

In the following chapters, we will examine the strengths and weaknesses of the Russian and Ottoman empires as they prepared for war.

---

1. B. Jelavich, *History of the Balkans*, (Cambridge 1983), p.113

Chapter Four

The Russian Empire

From the early days of Muscovy, Russia has faced challenges due to a poor strategic position. It was landlocked, had open borders without significant natural barriers, and was surrounded by numerous hostile neighbours. The climate, especially in winter, was extreme, and the short growing season, poor soil, and primitive agriculture left little surplus food for city development and trade. Despite these difficulties, Muscovy expanded through an autocratic government and military conquest. Instead of natural borders, it developed a system of client states that offered a partial buffer, particularly in the south and east. By importing Western technology, it created what Richard Hellie called 'a garrison state' and managed to dominate indigenous societies in the east and colonise large areas as far as Siberia and the Pacific Ocean.

Peter the Great

At the beginning of the 18th century, Russia was governed by Tsar Peter the Great (1672–1725). He became co-tsar with his half-brother, Ivan V, in 1682, with his sister, Sophia, acting as regent. Peter officially took complete control of the throne in 1696 after Ivan's death and Sophia's removal from power. He declared himself Emperor of Russia in 1721. Peter was a modernising ruler, reforming the state administration and adopting western customs and dress. He encouraged industry by establishing factories and promoting shipbuilding, and introduced tax reforms to increase state revenue. In 1703, he founded St. Petersburg, his 'window to the West,' and moved the capital there in 1714. His education reforms included establishing schools and academies to promote learning in sciences, engineering, and navigation, and he sent young Russians abroad to learn European technologies and governance practices. There was some internal opposition to these reforms from the traditional Russian nobility (boyars) and the Orthodox Church. However, he suppressed uprisings, such as the Streltsy Rebellion (1698) and Bulavin's Cossack Rebellion (1707), with brutal methods and a police state to maintain control.

His military reforms were shaped by Western advisors, including the Dutchman Franz Timmermann and the Catholic Scotsman Patrick Gordon, who arrived in Muscovy in 1661. Gordon became a full general in the Russian army, playing a key role in the capture of Azov from the Ottomans in 1696. Peter also famously travelled abroad, including to London, to study Western methods — the first tsar to leave Russia in a century. He established a standing army centred around his Preobrazhenskii and Semenovskii regiments, expanding to 27 'soldier' regiments and two regiments of dragoons. After the defeat at Narva (1700) by Sweden, Peter dismantled the remaining feudal troops, and by 1705, he commanded around 200,000 soldiers.

Peter's new army recovered from early defeats in the Great Northern War (1700–1721) despite losing his coalition partners, Saxony and Poland. Charles XII led the Swedish army and allies, including Cossacks under the Ukrainian Hetman Ivan Mazepa, south into Ukraine. This led to the decisive Battle of Poltava (27 June 1709), in which the exhausted and outnumbered Swedes were defeated. This victory shocked the world, with the writer Daniel Defoe commenting, 'An army of the bravest fellows in the world beaten by scoundrels.' The Swedish generals were more generous. Peter drank to the health of 'my teachers in war,' to which they responded, 'The pupils have delivered a good return to their masters.'[1]

Peter exploited the victory at Poltava by capturing key Baltic towns. However, he was dragged back south when the Ottomans, who had sheltered Charles XII after the Battle of Poltava, declared war in 1711. The Russians made a rash advance into Moldavia and were trapped against the Prut (Pruth) River. Peter was forced to make a costly peace, losing most of the gains made in 1699, including Azov. However, it could have been much worse if the Ottomans had taken advantage of their position. Peter recovered from this setback and, with a new coalition that included Britain, strengthened his position in the Baltic. The death of Charles in 1718 brought about peace negotiations and the Treaty of Nystad in 1721.

The enormous costs of the war didn't discourage Peter from further expansion in the Caucasus against Persia (1722–23) and in Central Asia. He also continued his reforms of the state and the military, including the establishment of a military code in 1716, which formed the basis of the Russian military for the remainder of this period. While these had their critics at home, where high taxes and conscription were unpopular, the transformation was noted abroad. A French diplomat concluded, 'Russia, whose very name was scarcely known, has now become the

---

1. C. Duffy, *Russia's Military Way to the West*, (Routledge, 1981), p.26.

object of attention of the greater number of the powers of Europe, who solicit its friendship.'[2] Peter I died on 8 February 1725.

Succession Crises 1725–41

Peter, for all his reforms, made no proper provision for his succession. He had killed off his only surviving son, Aleksei, in 1718 and abolished the principle of primogeniture. His second wife, Catherine I, succeeded to the throne, although real power was in the hands of the Supreme Privy Council. This continued when Catherine died in 1727 and was succeeded by Peter's grandson, Peter II (aged twelve), who died of smallpox in 1730. The Supreme Privy Council then picked Anna Ioannovna, a niece of Peter the Great who broke free of the Council and returned Russia to autocratic rule. She continued Peter's reforms and developed St. Petersburg, favouring Baltic Germans within the empire as her advisors. She also created a third guards regiment, the Ismailovskii, with many German officers and a regiment of Horse Guards. On her death in 1740, the infant Ivan IV became emperor under the regency of his mother Anna Leopoldovna (niece of Anna Ioannovna). His reign was short-lived due to a coup by Elizabeth Petrovna, Peter the Great's daughter, in 1741, restoring the direct Romanov line.

The leading military figure of this period was Burkhard Christoph von Münnich. Born into a noble family in Oldenburg, Germany, he trained as a military engineer and gained experience serving in the armies of France, Poland, and various German princes. He served under Prince Eugene and fought at the Battle of Malplaquet. He entered Russian service in 1721 under Peter the Great, who valued his engineering expertise. Promoted to General-in-Chief by Catherine in 1721, he modernised the Russian army by introducing Western tactics and engineering techniques, as well as new formations of cuirassiers and light cavalry (hussars), and doubled the number of regimental 3-pounder guns. The officer corps was reorganised, and he improved the discipline and training of Russian troops.

The Russian army campaigned in Poland, allied with the Austrians in 1733, but its primary test was the Russo-Ottoman War of 1735–1739. In 1736, Münnich captured the fortress of Azov, a key Ottoman stronghold at the mouth of the Don River. He led several expeditions into the Crimean Peninsula to neutralise the Crimean Khanate, but achieved little of lasting value due to disease and supply issues. In 1737, Münnich's forces captured the strategic fortress of Ochakov, controlling access to the southern Bug and Dniester rivers. This enabled one of the most celebrated feats of the war: crossing the heavily defended Dniester River and

---

2. C. Duffy, *Russia's Military Way to the West*, (Routledge, 1981), p.40.

launching operations deep into Ottoman territory, albeit with heavy losses. Austria entered the war in 1737 as Russia's ally, but faced multiple defeats at the hands of the Ottomans in the Balkans. Austria's poor performance eventually forced it to seek peace, undermining the Russian position. The Treaty of Belgrade (1739) secured Azov, but the Russians had to agree not to fortify it or maintain a naval presence in the Black Sea.

After the overthrow of Anna Leopoldovna's regency by Elizabeth Petrovna in 1741, Münnich was arrested and charged with treason. He was condemned to death but was later pardoned and exiled to Siberia, where he spent nearly 20 years. He regained his rank in 1762, but played no significant part in the subsequent war. Nevertheless, his reform of the Russian army into a more effective and modern force was vital to its success in later conflicts.

Elizabeth Petrovna

Elizabeth Petrovna was the second-eldest daughter of Peter the Great and Catherine I and took power in 1741, at the age of thirty-two, with the support of the Preobrazhensky Life Guards Regiment. Although judicial violence was still common, she notably did not sign a single death sentence. More significantly, she made education freely accessible to all social classes (except for serfs) and supported the establishment of the first university in Russia, in Moscow. She contributed to numerous construction projects in St. Petersburg, often funded by heavy taxation. She dismissed the German advisors, abolished the cabinet council system, and retreated from some of her father's religious reforms.

Foreign affairs were overseen by Aleksey Bestuzhev-Ryumin, who built alliances with Austria and Britain. A brief war with Sweden in 1742–43 saw Field Marshal Lacy (an Irish-born former Jacobite) defeat the Swedes in Finland, relying on a flotilla of galleys to supply his troops. The Treaty of Abo in 1743 established a sixty-mile buffer zone to protect against Swedish attacks.

The main military event of Elizabeth's reign was the Seven Years' War (1756–63), which involved Russia, Austria, and France opposing Frederick the Great of Prussia, who was supported by Britain. Elizabeth harboured a deep hatred for Frederick, and she often kept together the constantly conflicting elements of the anti-Prussian coalition. The Russian army was again reformed with a new infantry code devised by the court favourite, Petr Shuvalov. The cavalry was also reorganised, although the reforms made little progress by the time war broke out, and Russian horses were too light for the duties of heavy cavalry.

The main Russian commanders, Apraksin and Rumyantsev, invaded East Prussia and defeated the Prussians at the Battle of Gross-Jägersdorf (30 August 1757). However, Apraksin did not exploit the victory, and withdrew. His replacement was

General Wilhelm Fermor, who occupied East Prussia. Frederick responded to the Russian advance to the Oder by defeating the Russians at Zorndorf (25 August 1758), although both armies suffered heavy casualties, and Frederick had to march away to fight the Austrians. The following year, a combined Russian-Austrian army led by Pyotr Saltykov inflicted a catastrophic defeat on Frederick the Great's forces. The Battle of Kunersdorf (12 August 1759) was one of Frederick's worst defeats, although again the coalition failed to exploit the victory. In 1760, a column of Russian troops briefly captured Berlin, and the following year, they captured Kolberg, cutting off Prussia's access to the Baltic.

Elizabeth's health began to decline in the late 1750s. She suffered a stroke on 24 December 1761 and died the next day. Because she had no children, Elizabeth had brought Peter the Great's grandson, Peter, to Russia from Holstein in 1742 as heir presumptive. She married him to Sophia, who converted to Orthodoxy and took the name Ekaterina (Catherine). Peter III admired Frederick the Great and withdrew Russia from the war, signing the Treaty of Saint Petersburg in May 1762. Russia's exit prevented Prussia from potential collapse and marked a turning point in the conflict.

However, many in the Russian army resented having to hand back territories gained at such great cost. Empress Catherine herself feared that if Peter continued his concessions to Prussia, it would lead to a nationwide uprising and threaten Russia's stability. In the spring of 1762, conspiring with her lover Grigory Orlov and others in the court and military, Catherine overthrew her husband. Peter officially died of a stroke, but he was probably murdered.

Catherine II (the Great)

Catherine was born on 2 May 1729 in Stettin, Prussia, as Princess Sophie Augusta Frederica von Anhalt-Zerbst-Dornburg. Anhalt-Zerbst was one of around three hundred German-speaking principalities scattered around modern Germany. A few hundred square miles of pine forests and pastureland were squeezed between Saxony to the south and Prussia to the north. Once proudly independent, the impoverished rulers had served in the Prussian army for several generations, including Sophie's father, Prince Christian August, who was the governor of Stettin when she was born.

Sophie was a clever, brash child who, when in the presence of Frederick the Great, asked, 'Why does the king have such a short jacket? He's rich enough to afford a longer one, isn't he?' Frederick, not known for a sense of humour, actually laughed,

'The little one is impertinent.'[3] She received her education primarily from a French governess and from tutors specialising in etiquette, French, and Lutheran theology. According to her memoirs, Sophie was considered a tomboy and trained herself to master a sword. She also challenged her tutors, particularly her religious tutor. Her mother, Johanna, doted on her son and despaired of Sophie, whom she deemed 'highly intelligent, pleasing but plain.'

A good marriage was the primary role of German princesses, and several were suggested before Sophie and her mother were invited to Russia. Sophie ingratiated herself with the Empress Elizabeth, learned some Russian, and when she fell ill with pleuritis, she requested an Orthodox priest. Sophie converted to the Russian Orthodox Church and took the new name Catherine (Ekaterina). Catherine and Peter married in Saint Petersburg on 21 August 1745. Catherine had recently turned sixteen.

Peter and Catherine (Grooth)

The marriage was unsuccessful and likely remained unconsummated for several years. They had a son, Paul (later Paul I), in 1754, although he may have been the product of Catherine's first lover, Sergi Saltykov. They also had a daughter, Anna, in 1759, who only lived for fourteen months. Peter had taken a mistress, and Catherine had lovers, engaging in court politics and eventually living apart from her husband. Catherine had been involved in plots against Elizabeth, with the likely aim of later removing Peter, since at least 1749. He might have been planning to divorce her and send her to a convent when he became emperor. Catherine described her options in her memoirs: 'I could perish with him, or at his command, or else save myself, my children and perhaps the state from the shipwreck which threatened.' As we have seen, she forced Peter to abdicate (he subsequently died) after a reign of only 186 days, with the support of the guard's regiments and her lover Grigory Orlov.

Catherine was crowned at the Assumption Cathedral in Moscow on 22 September 1762. Unlike her predecessors, Catherine was diligent and industrious. She revitalised the Senate as the primary governing body, ably supported by her foreign minister, Nikita Panin (in office 1763–1781). Panin was Catherine's political men-

---

3. C. Erickson, *Great Catherine*, (Simon & Schuster, 1994), p.1.

tor during the first eighteen years of her reign, although tensions arose over policy, and she never appointed him as Chancellor. He also served as the governor of her heir, Paul, which gave him further influence at court.

Peter the Great was the guiding influence behind Catherine's approach to ruling the Russian Empire. She aimed to restore Peter the Great's 'regulated state' and even carried a snuffbox decorated with his portrait wherever she went. She planned to continue his reforms, which had stalled during the reign of his successors. In some ways, she went further by engaging in lengthy correspondence with Voltaire and encouraging the Russian intelligentsia to question old dogmas. These included promoting population growth and abolishing the maiming and torture of prisoners, with capital punishment reserved for murder. She wrote that the government should 'shun all occasions of reducing people to a state of slavery.' However, serfs in Russia lived under conditions very similar to slavery, and she was persuaded against implementing significant reforms. Her visit to the Volga region in 1767 convinced her that Russian laws needed reform, which led to the formation of a Legislative Commission composed of representatives from all estates. However, she lost patience with the process and dissolved it the following year. The Russian autocracy reasserted itself as war with the Ottomans drew near.

When it came to medical reform, Catherine was the only reigning monarch to undergo inoculation for smallpox—an act of courage that has since been largely forgotten. She invited the British doctor, Thomas Dimsdale, to Russia to perform the procedure, which could have had incalculable consequences had it gone wrong.[4] Dimsdale's wife, Elizabeth, kept a journal of her visit to St Petersburg in 1781, which included a demonstration of the game of cricket to Grand Duke Paul.[5] Sadly, the game never caught on in Russia.

While Catherine was interested in new ideas, there were other immediate challenges to be addressed. The Seven Years' War had almost bankrupted the state, and the army had not been paid for eight months. There were plots against her, and the two main political factions (Panin and Bestuzhev/Orlov) had to be balanced in the governing Senate. The nobles had welcomed Peter III's decree exempting them from compulsory state service, and they waited to see how Catherine would proceed. The church was less enthusiastic when she confiscated ecclesiastical property, reducing the number of monasteries from 572 to 161 and convents from 217 to 67.[6] She started by reining in state spending, including the military, although it rarely fell below half the net budget, even in peacetime. She expanded the scope of

---

4. L. Ward, *The Empress and the English Doctor*, (One World, 2022).

5. A. Cross, (Ed.), *An English Lady at the Court of Catherine the Great*, (Crest, 1989).

6. S. Dixon, *The Modernisation of Russia*, (Cambridge, 2012), p. 68.

the *Soul Tax* (Poll tax on peasant communes) and increased the rate and scope of the *Obrok* rent on state peasants. These were the two main taxes, and by 1765, she had paid off the debt and built up a significant financial reserve. She also lifted duties on grain exports and took greater control of the revenue from the state monopolies on salt and liquor. Despite these reforms, the forthcoming war with the Ottomans would require loans from abroad. Around five million roubles were borrowed to finance the war from bankers in Amsterdam, half of which was repaid from the Ottoman indemnity payments. Military success reduced the cost of borrowing, and a further 39 million roubles were borrowed between 1787 and 1792. The printing of paper money, initially a temporary measure during the Seven Years' War, became the norm, with significant inflationary consequences.

Russia was a vast country to administer from the centre. Peter the Great had introduced regional governorates above the old towns and districts. Catherine created new governorates (raising the number to twenty-three) in the expanding empire, particularly Ukraine. She outlined the duties of governors in her *Precept to Governors* and attempted to reduce bribery and corruption by establishing a system of salaries and pensions. However, there was a shortage of educated officials at the middle level, exacerbated by the nobility being freed from compulsory service.

Catherine II died in 1796, widely celebrated for modernising Russia and establishing the empire as a global player. However, Catherine fell victim to numerous rumours spread by her enemies, in the court and beyond. Many of her nobles clung to their resentment over how she had come to the throne, as well as the fact that she was not Russian at all. In the salons of Western Europe, it was joked that the government of Russia was a despotism tempered by assassination. She was painted as a nymphomaniac with an insatiable desire for young men, and while she did have an active sex life, it was no more adventurous than that of male rulers and nobles of the period. Catherine received similar treatment to other powerful women throughout history who have dared to have a sex life. And no, contrary to the widely propagated myth, she did not meet a lurid death during an attempt at bestiality with a horse![7] She suffered a stroke in her washroom and died aged sixty-seven. It could be argued that Catherine was a lucky monarch. The Ottomans were at their weakest for a generation, Austria and Prussia could be played off against each other, and Britain and France were distracted by the American War of Independence. This enabled her to reorient her policy towards expansion in the south.

She was an autocrat, but there were limitations, and she did not ignore public opinion. One of Potemkin's aides related a conversation with her about how her will was being fulfilled everywhere. She responded, 'It is not as easy as you think...I take advice, I consult the enlightened part of my people, and in this way I find out

---

7. J. Wilkes, *Did Catherine the Great really have sex with a horse?* (History Extra, 14 Feb. 2025).

what sort of effect my laws will have. And when I am already convinced in advance of good approval, then I issue my orders, and have the pleasure of observing what you call blind obedience.'[8]

The Steppe Frontier

As the Russian state expanded south towards the Black Sea region, a system of military colonisation developed. While this was largely successful in defending against Tatar incursions, it didn't allow for the normal development of this rich agricultural region, with troop levies and taxation becoming increasingly onerous. The defence line moved south as the frontier expanded following earlier wars against the Ottomans. Still, there were few incentives for peasants (*odnodvortsy*) or the nobility to exploit the regions now free from raiding.

The other military inhabitants of the southern frontier were the Cossacks. Those wanting to avoid serfdom or taxation could move to the border and seek to join the Don Cossack Host. Some Cossacks may have been former galley slaves of the Tatars and Ottomans who escaped and made their way to the Steppe frontier. Young people from noble families could join for brief periods, hence the phrase 'went cossacking,' before settling down.[9] The Host operated semi-independently under its own elected *ataman*, with a headquarters at Monastyrskii, 60 kilometres from the Ottoman fortress at Azov. They made their own raids on the Tatars and made sea raids along the Black Sea coast. Moscow recognised their value by sending an annual subsidy payment (*starshina*), which became increasingly important as the population grew without the means to support itself. After the Razin Revolt (1670–71), Moscow started to regulate the flow of refugees and the Host generally, along with Russian garrisons in the border forts. While this worked in the lower Don, the Upper Reaches were still liable to revolt, which drew further reorganisation. By 1738, the Ataman of the Host was appointed by and answerable to St Petersburg, and Cossacks were registered and liable for universal military service.

---

8. R. Massie, *Catherine the Great: Portrait of a Woman* (Head of Zeus, 2012), p. 572.

9. J. Wieczynski, *The Russian Frontier,* (University of Virginia, 1976), p.66.

Reply of the Zaporozhian Cossacks (Repin)

The Hetmanate on the Left Bank of Ukraine (east of the Dnieper, including Kyiv) had joined forces with the Swedes against Peter the Great, under the leadership of Hetman Ivan Mazepa. Their defeat led to closer Russian regulation and the appointment of Russian loyalist Kyrilo Rozumovsky in 1750. The finances of the Hetmanate were strictly controlled along with troop levies. Rozumovsky overreached himself by asking Catherine for greater autonomy in 1763, and was dismissed the following year. He was replaced by Rumyantsev, who had distinguished himself in the Seven Years' War. He was instructed to integrate Ukraine into the Empire, which included the introduction of serfdom and taxation into Ukraine in 1766. Cossack colonels were incorporated into the nobility, and a new 'rouble tax' replaced the provisioning in kind of Russian regiments, doubling the revenue raised from Ukraine. A similar process was adopted in Sloboda Ukraine (northeastern Ukraine and southwestern Russia), which resulted in its dissolution by 1765, and its Cossack regiments were replaced with hussar regiments. The Zaporozhian Cossack Host was also incorporated and effectively abolished during our period. The Cossack elite accepted these reforms because they maintained their local power on new terms. They were also allowed to claim land and peasants, secure appointments in the Russian system, and even pursue imperial careers, thereby gaining a new status as nobles. 'Many Cossacks found that the end of traditional rights associated with Little Russia was amply compensated by the opening of new horizons in Great

Russia.'[10] For those outside the elite in Ukraine, the reforms turned peasants into serfs, and the Jews were expelled from Kyiv.

The Russians also experimented with a system of military colonists, modelled after the Habsburg Grenzer system. A Serbian adventurer, Ivan Horvat, was assigned lands sufficient to sustain four regiments of 4,000 men each, to be recruited from disaffected Serbs. However, the Habsburgs addressed their grievances and banned emigration. The special status of 'New Serbia' as it became known created internal tensions, and Catherine abandoned the scheme in 1765, dispersing the several thousand immigrants into the general population.[11]

As the Russian border edged south, it also impinged on traditional nomadic tribal groups who lived on the Steppe. The Kalmyks were originally a nomadic group of Oirat-speaking Mongols who migrated from Western Mongolia into the lower Volga region on the northwest shore of the Caspian Sea. They were a significant military power at the start of the eighteenth century, courted by the Russians and the Ottomans. However, Russian fortifications began to encroach on the Kalmyk borders, cutting them off from their traditional pasturelands. In 1724, on the death of Ayuki Khan, the Russians abolished the Khanate and appointed their own Kalmyk loyalist, Dorji-Nazar, as viceroy. However, this backfired when he refused the appointment, and the Russians recognised the risk that the Kalmyks might join the Crimean Khanate or emigrate eastwards. The Russians temporarily compromised, but the expansion of colonisation and control of trade undermined Kalmyk unity through a series of civil wars. When the Russians insisted that they provide 20,000 troops for the war, most of the Kalmyks migrated to Chinese territories. A Russian-educated and appointed leader, Prince Dondukov, controlled those who remained. The Khanate was formally abolished in 1771 and subjected to regulation by the Russian Kalmyk Administration.[12]

To the east of the Kalmyks were the Kazakhs, divided into three hordes that together could field 100,000 cavalry. The Lesser Horde's proximity to the Russian frontier brought them into conflict with the Russian-dominated Bashkirs and the Kalmyks. In 1731, a treaty was agreed in which they pledged loyalty to the Tsar and agreed to protect caravans travelling to Russian-controlled Astrakhan. This was not without internal tensions, but it enabled the Russians to expand their territory while playing the tribes off against each other.

Russian policy in the years leading up to the Russo-Ottoman War of 1768 was to centralise the disparate frontier societies into a cameral system of control. As Pro-

---

10. D. Lieven, *The Cambridge History of Russia*, Vol. 2, (Cambridge, 2006), p.170.

11. W. McNeill, *Europe's Steppe Frontier*, 1500–1800, (Chicago, 1964), pp.191-192.

12. M. Khodarkovsky, *Russia's Steppe Frontier*, (Indiana Press, 2004), pp.133-146.

fessor Brian Davies put it, 'Thus policy initially acknowledged and accommodated differences but treated these differences as temporary, eventually surmounted to achieve uniformity and integration.'[13] The continued independence of the Cossack and tribal entities was no longer worth the trouble they caused.

---

13. B. Davies, *The Russo-Turkish War, 1768-1774*, (Bloomsbury, 2016), p.83.

Chapter Five

The Ottoman Empire

By the start of the eighteenth century, the Ottoman Empire had reached its apogee, but it was still holding its own on the battlefield. The Ottoman administrative system in the eighteenth century was characterised by both continuity and adaptation, reflecting the challenges and complexities of governing a vast and diverse empire. This period, marked by a gradual decline in central authority, saw significant changes in how the empire managed its territories.

Administration

The central administration was based around the sultan, who remained the supreme ruler and the ultimate source of authority. From 1757, this was Sultan Mustafa III. In an earlier period, he would not have lived to become sultan. In 1730, after a mob uprising (the Patrona Halil Revolt) led to the deposition of his father, Sultan Ahmed III, and the succession of his cousin, Sultan Mahmud I, Mustafa, his father, and his brothers were imprisoned in the Topkapı Palace. In 1756, after the death of his elder half-brother, Mehmed, he became the heir and then the Sultan following the death of his cousin, Osman III. Mustafa was an admirer of Frederick the Great and signed a peace treaty with Prussia in 1761, aimed at curbing the power of the Habsburgs. He looked to Prussia for help with his military reforms.

By the eighteenth century, the sultan's influence had waned in practice, with a growing reliance on influential advisors and officials, particularly the grand vizier. The grand vizier acted as the de facto head of state and often wielded significant authority in decision-making. There were nine grand viziers during Mustafa's reign, and six during the Russo-Ottoman War. None of them served for more than a year, other than Muhsinzade Mehmed Pasha (from 1771 to 1774). According to Stanford Shaw, a historian who specialised in Turkish history, the only vizier of any consequence during Mustafa's reign was Koca Ragıp Pasha (Koca means 'great' or 'giant' in Turkish), who served from 1757 until he died in 1763. He was an experienced and able administrator who reformed the finances, kept the Ottomans out of the Seven Years' War, and had a close working relationship with Mustafa.

Sultan Mustafa III

The Divan, an advisory council, lost influence as governance shifted to the vizier's office and bureaucratic mechanisms took hold. The Sublime Porte became the centre of Ottoman administrative activity, featuring a professional bureaucracy that included scribes and officials managing complex record-keeping and correspondence. However, it developed on a smaller scale compared to its western opponents. European war and naval ministries, staffed by professional administrators, helped develop the capacity and capability to wage war through everything from weapons improvement to training to ensuring the supply of weapons, food, and fodder. Improvements in technology, organisation, and logistics owed much to these ministries, which had only partial Ottoman counterparts.

The empire was divided into *eyalets* (provinces) governed by pashas, who represented the central authority. Each *eyalet* was subdivided into *sanjaks* (districts), managed by *sanjak-beys* (sub-governors). The provincial administration became increasingly reliant on *iltizam* (tax farming) in which individuals or groups bid to collect taxes on behalf of the state, resulting in economic inefficiencies and corruption. The traditional *timar* system (land grants to *sipahi* cavalry in exchange for military service) declined significantly. The decentralisation of power allowed local power holders, including *ayan* (notables) and tribal leaders, to gain significant autonomy. Economic grievances, inflation, and corruption led to revolts in provinces, further weakening central control.

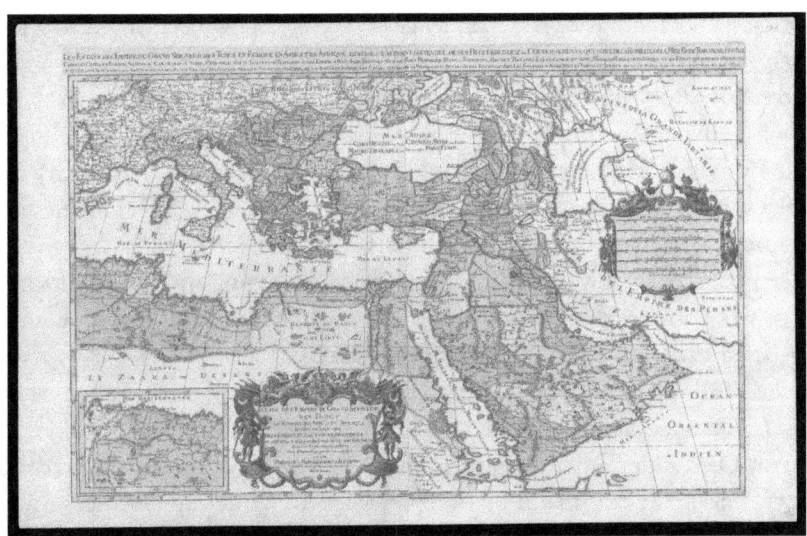

Provinces of the Ottoman Empire in 1692 by Guillaume Sanson

The *ulema* (Islamic scholars) and the *Shaykh al-Islam* (religious advisory council) played a central role in interpreting and implementing Islamic law (*Sharia*). They often served as a conservative counterbalance to reform efforts. Non-Muslim communities (*dhimmis*) were governed by their religious leaders and laws under the millet system, maintaining a degree of autonomy in personal and communal matters.

The Empire's approach to war

Any decline in the Ottoman Empire was not immediately apparent in the first half of the eighteenth century. Peter the Great had been humbled in the Prut Campaign of 1711, and the Venetians had been cleared from the Morea (modern Peloponnese in Greece) in 1715. There was a significant setback against Prince Eugene and the Austrians in 1717, but ground was recovered when the Ottomans defeated the Austrians in the 1736–39 war, particularly at Belgrade. As we have seen, the Russians gained little from their campaigns on the steppe frontier. Outside Europe, a protracted conflict with Persia in the 1720s and 1730s was only settled in 1747.

The Habsburgs were mainly left on the defensive in the Balkans, as they faced wars in the west and the rise of Prussia. They also had to incorporate territorial gains in Italy and the Banat (modern-day northwestern Romania and northeastern Serbia) into the empire. The multilingual empire also faced internal challenges, including Rákóczi's War of Independence (1703–1711), which sought to separate Hungary from the Habsburgs.[1]

Successful campaigns encouraged conservative elements to resist reforms. However, local elites increasingly carried the burden of border conflicts and gained autonomy as a consequence. This would be accelerated later in the century under notables such as Ali Pasha and Osman Pasvanoglu. Historians differ in their view of the impact of this decentralisation. Some argue it weakened military effectiveness, while a more recent view is that the changes had economic and military logic. Tax farming was a logical response to the commercialisation of the economy, and the *timar*-based *sipahi* cavalry was tactically obsolete.

In the 1737 war against the Austrians, the Bosnian army, commanded by Hekimoğlu Ali Pasha, quickly mobilised to defend against the Austrian invasion, while the main Ottoman field army slowly made its way to Vidin in the traditional manner, under the command of the grand vizier. While the distances involved created logistical challenges for the Ottomans, significant progress had been made in improving communications through a programme of bridge building. However, military reform was slower, and we will cover that in a later chapter. Suffice it to say that the long period of relative peace between 1747 and 1768 was not used effectively, even though economic recovery was achieved.

The Russian frontier and the Balkans

North of the Danube, the border with Russia was Wallachia and Moldavia. Before the Prut Campaign of 1711, these were vassals of the Sultan with significant autonomy, including their own troops for border defence. However, when they welcomed Peter the Great, the Ottoman response was to replace the local rulers (*Hospodar*) with Greek officials known as *Phanariots*, named after Phanar, the Greek quarter of Constantinople. While the Phanariots had their guard troops, the border defence relied on Ottoman fortresses, such as Khotyn (Khotin) in northern Moldavia (modern Ukraine), the Tatar hordes in Bessarabia, and the fortress of Bender in eastern Moldavia. The Phanariot system relied heavily on tax farming, which trebled the tax burden in Moldavia between 1714 and 1750. As a consequence, peasants fled into Ottoman or Austrian territory, halving the population of peasants in Wallachia. Others turned to banditry as *Hajduks* or revolted. These problems did not go unnoticed by the Ottoman government, but the extra revenue trumped these concerns, and they had direct control of the border defences.

---

1. For Austria in this period see M. Hochedlinger, *Austria's Wars of Emergence, 1683–1797*, (Longman, 2003).

Bordering Russian Ukraine was the region of Bucak with the Tigheci Hills to the north and the Dniester River in the east. This was a sparsely populated region defended by Ottoman fortresses, including Akkerman (modern Bilhorod-Dnistrovskyi, Ukraine), Bender, Ismail and Özi (Ochakov, modern Ochakiv). The Nogai Horde had migrated to this steppe, and although nominally vassals of the Ottomans, they were difficult to control. The Russians also took advantage of opportunities to recruit them into their service.

The traditional threat to Russia came from the Tatars of the Crimean Khanate, an Ottoman vassal since 1475. The khan and the two other leadership positions (the Kalga Sultan and Nureddin Sultan) were traditionally held by the Giray family, which claimed descent from Cingiz Khan. Therefore, they all bore the epithet *Cingiziye*. The Khanate encompassed the Crimean Peninsula and vast swathes of steppe from Transylvania to the Caucasus, loosely ruled from its capital, Bakhchysarai. Income came from the towns and other lands, supplemented by the Ottomans. The administration was similar to that of the Ottoman government, with Muslim institutions, clans, the Nogai Horde, and the Ottoman *sanjak* of Kaffa (Feodosia) operating largely independently of the khan. The clans appointed their own leaders, although the khan nominally approved them. The Nogai Horde was a nomadic people who considered their way of life superior to that of the settled populations in Crimea and frequently rebelled against them. There were also non-Muslim minorities living in separate communities in southern Crimea.[2]

By the eighteenth century, the massive Tatar slave raids had diminished, although a raid on the lower Volga in 1717 took 30,000 prisoners. These were sold at the slave markets at Kaffa, with many being sold into the Ottoman Empire. However, the large Tatar forces that traditionally screened the Ottoman army were in decline, possibly numbering as few as 50,000 to 70,000 men. This was due to Cossack raids reducing their revenue and military advances, including the use of artillery and increased firepower, as well as the strengthening of the Russian fortress line. When the Russians held the fortresses at Kazikermen (modern Beryslav) and Azov, the Khanate was cut off. In the 1736–39 Russo-Ottoman War, the Russians had pushed deep into the Crimea. Following that war, the Crimean khans avoided conflict with the Russians, which suited the Ottoman foreign policy of peace with Christian Europe. The khan even accepted a Russian consul to the Crimea in 1763, to develop trade. However, he fell out with the khan in 1765 and was expelled.

To the east of Crimea was the Kuban steppe and the northern Caucasus. The Crimean Khanate's control of this area had been declining as the Russians advanced down the Volga. They had conquered Astrakhan at the north end of the Caspian Sea in 1556, and Cossack colonies had moved south along the western Caspian Sea

---

2. A. Fisher, *The Russian Annexation of the Crimea* (Cambridge, 1970), Ch. 1.

coast. The local tribes, including the Kuban Horde and the Kabardians, began to seek alliances with the Russians. Peter the Great had used the collapse of the Persian Safavid dynasty as an excuse to invade the Caucasus in 1722, establishing garrisons along the Terek River and reaching a treaty with the new Persian state in 1732. The northern Caucasus was involved in the Russo-Ottoman war of 1735 when Crimean Tatars and Kuban Nogais fought against Russians, Cossacks, Kalmyks, and some Kabardians. The treaty ending the war stipulated that Kabardia was to remain independent, although this did not stop raids by both sides.

Peter the Great recognised the benefits of stirring up religious issues in the Ottoman Balkans, which were predominantly populated by Orthodox Christians. This had been a factor in his advance into Moldavia, although fewer joined his army than the *hospodars* promised. He had also reached out to the Montenegrins, who had achieved a degree of autonomy within the Ottoman Empire, hoping this might give the Russians access to the Adriatic. Diplomatic exchanges continued up to the 1760s, when Colonel Puchkov was sent to Montenegro to report on the possibilities. He advised not to get involved as corruption siphoned off Russian financial assistance to the church, and 'the people are wild, they live in disorder, heads roll for the least offence.'[3] In 1766, an impostor claiming to be Catherine the Great's dead husband, Peter III, managed to assume power as Stephen the Small, which stopped any outside support. As late as 1777, the Montenegrin mission to St. Petersburg was not received by Catherine. However, when the 1787 war broke out, both the Austrians and the Russians sent military advisors and gifts. The Ottomans launched fresh attacks on the Montenegrins, although as the British ambassador to Constantinople reported in October 1768, 'I am told the Montenegrins are joined by different bodies of mountaineers more numerous than themselves, which will cause time and great expense to subdue them.'[4] This would become a regular pattern in Ottoman efforts to bring the Montenegrins under their control.

The Albanians were less open to external influence, as they had some of the largest numbers of conversions to Islam. They were incentivised to convert through the tax system, but that applied elsewhere. Unlike the Orthodox Church, the Catholic Church, which concentrated mainly in the north of the country, was not accommodated in the Ottoman system because it was viewed as a major enemy. Albanian Muslims had numerous opportunities to serve the Ottoman state, as they were highly valued for their military skills and were employed throughout the empire. They often served as the personal guards of notables. Many Janissaries originated from Albanian families, and up to thirty men of Albanian background served as

---

3. B. Davies, *The Russo-Turkish War, 1768-1774*, (Bloomsbury, 2016), p.34.

4. The National Archives: FO 110/86, *Sir John Murray to Foreign Office*.

grand viziers.⁵ Serving abroad did not mean Albania was left a peaceful place. Local notables fought amongst themselves, coalescing into two power blocs by the end of the century: the Bushati family, led latterly by Kara Mahmud (Mahmud Bushati) in the north, and Ali Pasha of Janina (Ioannina) in the south. Kara Mahmud is less well-known than the famous Ali Pasha. Still, he fought successful campaigns against Montenegrin bandits and brought the Dalmatian colonies of the Republic of Venice under Ottoman tribute. He would play an important role in defeating the Greek revolt in the coming war, as well as against the Austrians in 1790–1.⁶

Albanian bandits have been described as 'social bandits' to distinguish them from proto-revolutionary 'national' bandits such as the *klephts* in Greece. Anscombe asserts that Albanian (Muslim) bandits were, above all, motivated by the profit that plundering could bring them rather than by any particular ideology.⁷ Many Albanians turned to brigandage (in comparison to other population groups) due to environmental and socioeconomic conditions in the lands populated by Albanians, including low agricultural productivity as well as the rise of large farms (*çiftliks*), which led to increasing peasant indebtedness.

South of the Danube lay Bulgaria, divided into five *sanjaks*, and it had significantly less local autonomy than other parts of the Balkans. The long period of peace had strengthened the Bulgarian economy, with internal trade and exports expanding across the Danube and through the Black Sea port of Varna. It had a significant Muslim minority, and the revolts of the 1680s were not repeated in this period.

With Greeks holding high positions in the Ottoman administration, and Greek merchant shipping benefiting from the long period of peace, the provinces that encompass modern Greece had remained relatively quiet. It also had a degree of autonomy in local government, and Greek notables profited from the system. However, Greek peasants were taxed heavily and had to relinquish a large proportion of their output to Ottoman and Greek landlords. The Mani Peninsula in the Morea had only just been recovered from the Venetians in 1715, and large numbers of its inhabitants belonged to armed bands, known as *klephts* or *armatoles*. These were little more than bandits, even if often romanticised in Greek historical writing. Russia was making some efforts to build an intelligence network in the region, which would later pay dividends.

---

5. B. Jelavich, *History of the Balkans*, (Cambridge 1983), p. 81.

6. O. Jazexhi, *Kara Mahmud Pasha Bushati: The Buffalo of Shkodra*, (Dielli, 2021).

7. F. Anscombe, *Albanians and Mountain Bandits: The Ottoman Balkans, 1750–1830*, (Princeton, 2006).

Like Albania, Bosnia and Herzegovina had a large-scale conversion to Islam, which led to a Muslim ruling class of Slavic origin, while only constituting a third of the population. They provided an effective border force against the Habsburgs to the north and were a large part of Ottoman armies elsewhere. This was the scene of heavy fighting in the wars against Austria, and the economy suffered greatly. The Serbs had not converted in significant numbers, and the Muslim population was concentrated in cities. The Serbian Orthodox Church regarded the Catholic Habsburgs as its main rival and was accommodated in the Ottoman system. The rural Serbs had been drawn into past conflicts by appeals from Austria and later Russia, and this had led to migration across the border. They were not involved in the 1768 war, but they volunteered in their thousands in 1788. However, they felt abandoned at the end of the war, leaving a legacy of distrust of the Habsburgs. Some 50,000 refugees were allowed to return, many of whom had military experience and would play a role in the rebellions of the next century.

The ancient Republic of Ragusa (Dubrovnik) on the Dalmatian coast was nominally independent, although in practice an Ottoman protectorate until 1806. It operated for the Ottomans in a similar way to Hong Kong, linking trade routes from Western Europe into the empire.

Ottoman Economy

The Ottoman Empire was under pressure internally and externally before the 1768 war. However, the only Balkan territory they had lost was the Banat. Unlike the Russians, who were centralising power, the Ottomans had decentralised their empire. This had brought some economic benefits, and Ottoman finances were in better shape. Changes in landholding were significant, as the *timarlis* were not only soldiers but also administrators. No new group was brought in to replace them, but the *ulema*, Christian clergy, merchants, tax farmers, and local strong families became much more influential. However, the scale and pace of reform were slow, and this would make it difficult for the empire to respond to the challenges a new war would bring. In Russia, the population was growing, and tax revenues tripled between 1724 and 1769. This contrasts with a stable population of around 22 million in the Ottoman Empire, and revenues that only increased by 10 per cent.[8] Annual state expenditure rose by 30 per cent between 1761 and 1785; however,

---

8. G. Agostan, *Military Transformation in the Ottoman Empire and Russia, 1500–1800*, (Kritika: Explorations in Russia and Eurasian History, 12:2, Spring 2011), p.309.

during the war years, there was a 100 per cent increase. Soldiers' salaries comprised 75 per cent of expenditure in 1784, and 74 per cent by 1785.[9]

Ottoman rule in the Balkans is often denigrated in modern nationalist historiography, which claims that it limited educational and economic development. However, during this period, the rate of literacy in non-Ottoman lands was limited; serfs had few rights or means of self-expression, and rarely contributed to the governance of their countries. Agriculture in the Ottoman Empire used the same techniques as those in Western Europe, although the Ottomans had fallen behind in manufacturing and trade. As Peter Sugar concludes, 'The standard evaluations of Ottoman "backwardness" are exaggerated when applied to the end of the eighteenth century.'[10]

---

9. G. Agoston, J. Black ed., *European Warfare, 1453–1815*, (Macmillan, 1999), *Ottoman Warfare in Europe 1453–1826*, p.142.

10. P. Sugar, *Southeastern Europe under Ottoman Rule, 1354–1804*, (Washington, 1977), p.284.

Chapter Six

The Russian Army

Introduction

The Russian army of this period had its origins in the reforms instituted by Peter the Great at the start of the eighteenth century, which created a Western-style army with regular infantry, cavalry, and artillery. However, irregular forces, such as the Cossacks, were retained. Peter brought in foreign advisors, particularly from the Netherlands and Prussia, to train Russian officers and soldiers. European drill, linear tactics, and the use of flintlock muskets and bayonets were implemented. He also introduced conscription, requiring every twenty households to provide one soldier for lifelong service, and established military academies to train officers.

Peter's successors, particularly Empress Anna (1730–1740) and Elizabeth (1741–1762), continued his military policies, albeit with less intensity. The army was expanded and further professionalised through the work of the German Christoph Munnich. While he fell from grace, most of his reforms were retained, although an explicit policy of Russification replaced the Germanification of the army. The infantry remained the backbone of the army, with emphasis on discipline and massed volleys. Cavalry units, including cuirassiers and dragoons, were expanded for battlefield versatility. Artillery became a key component of Russian military power. Officers like Pyotr Shuvalov developed innovative artillery pieces. The subjugation of the peasants made it possible to draft and tax them as well as hold the nobility who owned them to account. This meant they could reinforce the ranks in a way that Western armies could not, allowing them to recover from extremely high casualty rates. The army was vast, but it needed to be so to defend the country's extensive borders and maintain internal security. The constant challenge was to find the means to pay for it. Savings were made by hiring out troops for work on estates, quartering them among the peasantry, where they grew their own food, and requiring the troops to manufacture some items of their own equipment.

Russo-Ottoman War 1735–1739

Munnich had the opportunity to test his reforms against the Ottomans during the 1735–39 war. The main strike was aimed at the fortresses defending the Crimea at Azov and Ochakov. The plan was then to move into Moldavia, claiming to free the Christians from Ottoman oppression. Whether Russian serfdom was a significant improvement for the peasants was a moot point.

Campaigns in the south required greater attention to supply. As early as 1732, Empress Anna had ordered the military administration of Ukraine to revisit the depots and to resupply and repair them, although the contractors directed supplies to the armies in Poland, leaving Munnich without the resources he needed for his ambitious plans.[1] The campaigns were not a great success, and as many as 60 per cent of Russian casualties were due to starvation, thirst, and disease. The lack of roads also hindered logistics, and while rivers could be utilised, the Ottoman forts at the mouths of the major rivers limited that option. Munnich doubled the number of logistics officers, but local governors retained their systems, and persistent corruption undermined already challenging logistics over vast distances. Unlike European campaigns, the territory being fought over had sparse populations and agricultural resources. The Russian baggage train could include at least 20,000 to 30,000 carts, which inevitably moved slowly.

Munnich gave careful thought to the balance of his forces, picking specific numbers for cavalry, infantry and artillery according to each army's primary objective—a raid, a siege, or a prolonged campaign with multiple tasks. Cavalry formed a much larger element of the armies in the south with regular dragoons, combining well with the irregular Cossacks and Kalmyks, and the two hussar regiments. Artillery played a vital role in the sieges of Azov and Ochakov, as well as in defending bases against Tatar attacks. However, it was the disciplined infantry that formed the backbone of the army, often fighting in large squares, to counter the Ottoman cavalry.

While the campaign achieved few gains, it did provide invaluable experience. They studied or captured the main Ottoman fortresses, gaining an understanding of the surrounding routes and terrain. Bulgarian historian A. Stoyanov concludes, 'In general, the Russians performed well, outmatching their enemies in every element of combat except for logistics. Russian troops were better in terms of firepower and precision, as well as in hand-to-hand combat. Colonels and captains were

---

1. A. Stoyanov, *Russia marches South: army reform and battlefield performance in Russia's Southern campaigns, 1695–1739*, (University of Leiden, 2017), p.205

brave and motivated, as well as tactically efficient, winning small-scale confrontations and defending positions with substantial ease and skill.'

Seven Years' War 1756–1763

With Munnich toppled, it was Petr Shuvalov who led the next stage of reforms that took the Russian army to the eve of the Seven Years' War. He reorganised the land militia and irregular forces, bringing the army up to a theoretical strength of around 350,000 men. However, with the need for garrisons, it still left around 220,000 men available to fight Prussia, the largest army in Europe at the time. The cavalry was a particular concern due to a shortage of mounts in the dragoon regiments. Shuvalov's artillery reforms delivered the largest artillery park in Europe with nearly 9,000 guns and 756 mortars, made possible by new mines and industrial production. Infantry regiments and dragoons had more regimental artillery, and the conical-barrelled 'unicorn' was half the weight of the standard regimental gun, allowing greater mobility while increasing its range. His slot-bored 'secret howitzer' could spread cannister across a wider arc. In 1755, a commission adopted new infantry regulations developed by Zakhar Chernyshev, which appeared to be a compromise between the Prussian system and the Petrine tradition. This included a three-line battle formation and gave the field commander a large number of possible combinations; for example, four types of regimental squares. However, 'Since it was impossible to impart drill for these and other complex evolutions within a short period, the Imperial Army fought the Seven Years' War primarily based on the old Petrine Statute and liberal improvisation.'[2]

Field Marshal Apraksin led 72,000 infantry, 7,000 cavalry, and 16,000 Cossacks against the Prussians. The army generally performed well, although the practice of taking a huge baggage train meant the army manoeuvred slowly, and needed large numbers of troops to protect it. Living off the countryside was possible in this region, but the Russians chose to maintain good relations with the Poles and Germans and paid for their supplies. As commanders gained more experience in Europe, they sought to establish permanent brigades and divisions; however, this was rejected as a deviation from Peter the Great's established practice. The exception was Shuvalov's Observation Corps, a combined arms formation that operated as a form of strategic reserve. However, it performed poorly at the battles of Zorndorf and Kunersdorf and was abolished in 1760. Commanders were allowed little initiative on campaign as the War Conference attached to the Imperial Court took control of almost all military matters.

---

2. B. Menning in *The Military History of Tsarist Russia*, (Palgrave, 2002), p. 52.

A series of organisational reforms was instituted in 1759. The baggage train was reduced by making greater use of waterways and local requisitioning in East Prussia. This allowed the army to divide into faster-moving columns, screened by large formations of Cossacks, now with regular officers, in an attempt to reduce indiscipline. More artillery was deployed on the front line, outgunning the Prussians. Frederick the Great found the resilience of Russian troops a considerable challenge, and after the Zorndorf and Kunersdorf battles, he said, 'I will not survive this...I have no more resources, and speaking frankly, I consider everything lost.'[3] He was spared, however, partly because the Russian army was forced to retire to winter quarters, and later by the death of the Empress and Peter III's withdrawal from the war.

Russian casualties in the war totalled around 120,000 men, of whom 97,000 died of disease. The experience of war in Europe had highlighted the mismanagement of supply, outdated training ordinances, and the centralisation of decision-making.

The Russian Army at the outset of the 1768 war

Catherine's immediate priority was to end Peter III's unpopular Prussian innovations, which included uncomfortable uniforms, and abandoning territorial designations, although that didn't involve returning to war with Prussia. In 1762, a special Military Commission, chaired by Petr Saltykov, was created, and published a range of reforms the following year that would create the structure to fight the Ottomans in 1768.

The standard infantry regiment would consist of two battalions, each of five musketeer companies and one grenadier company. Two reserve companies were held in quarters for the training of recruits. This created a fighting battalion of 800 men. The total size of the army was reduced to 104,000 men, in three guards, four grenadier, and 46 musketeer regiments. This was expanded to 63 regiments by incorporating most of the Ukrainian Land Militia into the regular army, allowing them to be deployed elsewhere, although they retained separate uniforms until 1779. Jägers had been introduced by Rumyantsev in 1761, and this innovation was expanded with small commands (60 men) in every infantry regiment by 1769. There were 48 garrison regiments of foot of generally poor-quality troops that were not regarded as a ready reserve for the field army.

---

3. B. Davies, *The Russo-Turkish War, 1768–1774*, (Bloomsbury, 2016), p.91.

Russian infantry

The 1763 infantry ordinances reduced the front line of an infantry battalion from four ranks to three, with the front line divided into four divisions and platoons, each consisting of eight to twelve ranks. Grenadier companies were placed on the flanks. The firing drill was simplified with the first two ranks firing from the knee, and the third rank standing at the ready. All ranks were required to have the bayonet attached. Firing was generally done by platoon, with ranks moving forward or back to fire, allowing the rear rank to stand and reload. This was becoming the standard in European armies. Battalions marched in column, but had not adopted the French practice of attack columns. Experience in fighting the Ottomans meant the Russian infantry was trained to form squares of battalion, regiment, or larger sizes with regimental guns on the corners. Cavalry and jägers were deployed in the gaps.

The cavalry was to be maintained on a ratio of one cavalry to two infantry, excluding the newly converted militia regiments. This meant 25 regiments of heavy cavalry, each of five squadrons, with two companies per squadron. The six regiments of cuirassiers were retained, but the mounted grenadiers were combined with 13 dragoon regiments to form 19 regiments of carabiniers. This reflected the European trend for heavier shock cavalry, and the remaining seven dragoon regiments were assigned to garrison duty. Light cavalry duties of reconnaissance and pursuit would be performed by hussars, *pikinier* lancers[4], and Cossacks. The six hussar regiments had six rather than five squadrons, and totalled 8,272 troopers. Cossack regiments and commands varied in numbers, but most came from the Don Host, which could mobilise 9,000 men. Smaller numbers came from the Volga, Iaik (Yaik), Greben,

---

4. *Pikinier* were named after the pikes they use, and were created in 1764 from military colonists in Ukraine and later Cossacks and peasants. They lost their Cossack privileges and were forced to remain in military service, pay taxes, and fulfil feudal obligations to the state.

and Azov hosts. Regular uniformed Cossacks were rare in this period, for they provided their own weapons and equipment. They wore long, woollen coats, with a busby replacing the cap, and were equipped with a lance, sword, dagger, pistols, and musket, of varying quality depending on their individual wealth.

These were supplemented by Kalmyk and other Asian tribespeople who retained traditional weapons, such as the bow. By 1763, the ordinance for cavalry emphasised shock over firepower. Carbine firing was generally to be undertaken dismounted in two ranks. Pistols could be fired mounted, but the focus was on the charge with cold steel.

The artillery had been one of the success stories of the Seven Years' War. Four three-pounder guns (or unicorn howitzers) were attached to every infantry regiment with a crew of eight men and six horses. There were five field artillery regiments, although these were administrative formations. The 350 guns were deployed in batteries of up to 24 guns, as required, using six-, eight-, and twelve-pounder guns.

Russian Dragoon, Cuirassier and Horse Grenadiers

They also had the unique Shuvalov 'secret howitzer,' which acted like a shotgun; slow to reload, but devastating when fired. The siege artillery trains were reduced to around 164 guns and mortars. Artillery crews were trained to fire at close range, keeping long-range fire to a minimum. There was an engineer regiment of three companies consisting of specialists, with infantry being lent for unskilled labour.

The Military Commission also reorganised the army administratively into eight divisions and three corps, assigning them to geographical regions. Each division had several regiments of infantry and cavalry organised into brigades commanded by a full general. Each regiment had its permanent quarters in a town or village. There was a limited experiment with combined arms legions of 5,667 troops, but this innovation did not survive the Ottoman War. The Commission also remade the old Quartermaster-General's department into a permanent General Staff. The War College gained influence under the presidency of Zakhar Chernyshev, who enjoyed weekly access to the Empress. Additionally, Chernyshev established a War Council in 1768 to oversee the war. However, military historian Christopher Duffy in particular questions how many of the reforms were fully implemented, equating them to the legendary 'Potemkin villages,' and tainted by corruption. From 1767, promotion was based on seniority, or as Duffy says, 'Seniority modified by corruption, and Catherine left her servants to enrich themselves as they sought fit from the resources at their command.'

The qualities of the rank-and-file Russian soldier commanded the most attention from foreign observers. A later observation by Count Langeron concluded that 'He is the finest soldier in the world.... He combines all the qualities which go to make a good soldier and a hero.'[5] There were seven million taxable males in the Russian Empire, and just 3.3 per cent were in military service. These numbers were obtained through conscription for twenty-five years because the nobility feared that the serfs would leave the land to join the army if voluntary enlistment were introduced. Some 40,000 could be called up each year, but this was often cancelled in peacetime or expanded during times of war. There were exceptions for priests and some other occupations, and buying a substitute was possible. Recruits had to be between seventeen and thirty-five years of age, at least five feet two inches tall, and have good teeth to bite open musket cartridges. Landowners selected the recruits, which meant they frequently offered the thieves, drunkards, and 'the feeblest person he can find.' During the war, Rumyantsev was 'shocked by the pitiable sight and deplorable waste of the recruits who straggled through to his army on the Turkish theatre, only to die from the first fatigues of military duty.'[6] Self-mutilation, hiding, and escaping were common means of avoiding conscription.

The pay was seven roubles fifty kopeks, free of deductions. There is some evidence that wives could follow husbands on campaign, although they were not on the regimental strength as per the later British practice. Garrisons were more regularised with garrison schools being introduced, not as a social reform, but rather to educate future NCOs. The soldier's family was his *artel*, a community of soldiers run by corporals, with four to a company, and they pooled resources, plunder, and other assets. From this, they supplemented their very basic rations. Punishments were formally no worse than those of other armed forces of the period, but they differed by the common practice of informal blows from NCOs and officers. Unsurprisingly, desertion was common. Religion was a binding factor, and many wore images of their patron saint around their necks.

Officers were recruited from the gentry (not always nobles, and certainly not all wealthy), which numbered around 100,000 males. Children could be enrolled as supernumerary soldiers at the age of thirteen, although they didn't serve until much later, usually at the time of war. Only a small proportion of leaders had followed a formal course of military education, despite the fact that such establishments had been established by Peter the Great on the Western model. The higher nobility

---

5. C. Duffy, *Russia's Military Way to the West*, (Routledge, 1981), p.125.

6. C. Duffy, *Russia's Military Way to the West*, (Routledge, 1981), p.129.

regarded it as too exacting. Shuvalov and Catherine strengthened the technical schools and increased the establishment. In addition, the Cadet Corps produced around fifty-five young men for the army and civilian service, again expanded by Catherine. This Corps provided a broader education, encompassing literature, foreign languages, and military subjects. The Table of Ranks established grades from the lowest (14) to the highest (1) at court. An army officer (grade 14 and higher) qualified for nobility, while those serving at court and in the bureaucracy had to advance up to grade 8 to qualify. The army was therefore the quickest route to social mobility, albeit a riskier one. The system delivered very mixed outcomes in terms of officer quality. 'Incompetence, mediocrity, peculation and even sadism were to be met with within Russia's eighteenth-century officer corps. There were, however, also officers who distinguished themselves by their honesty, fairness and paternalistic concern for the well-being of their men.'[7]

Catherine sought to restrict army commands (Field-Marshal) to native Russians, but the army still extensively recruited foreigners, as did other countries of the period. Non-native Russians constituted over 40 per cent of staff officers, including many senior commanders in the 1768 war. However, while most European armies employed men from many nationalities as well as mercenaries, the Russian infantry soldier was almost entirely recruited from the peasant levy. Russia maintained Europe's largest standing army on revenues that were one-fifth of those of France, with all male Russians (in theory) subject to conscription.

As Davies highlights, ordinances were useful for training purposes, but commanders in the field would adapt them in light of combat experience. The Prussian model was the prevailing doctrine, but Russian commanders were open to other ideas and recognised that Prussian tactics had their limitations when fighting the Ottomans. As Alexander Burns concludes in his study of infantry in battle, 'Infantry soldiers in the eighteenth century sometimes disobeyed their officers' commands and fought in a way that made sense to them. They aimed their weapons, fought as skirmishers, and fired independently and uncontrolled, often at a greater range than their officers preferred.'[8]

In the coming war, Russian commanders would innovate tactically to reflect the nature of warfare on the steppe. They would concentrate forces rather than trying to hold a long defensive line, and seek out battle, taking the offensive into Ottoman territory. Staged offensives allowed shorter supply lines with smaller forces moving quickly in flying raids. The army would advance in parallel columns rather than as Munnich's one large army, allowing forced marches. Columns became part of the

---

7. W. Fuller, D. Lieven, Ed., *The Cambridge History of Russia, Vol. 2*, (Cambridge, 2006), p. 535.

8. A. Burns, *Infantry in Battle, 1733–1783*, (Helion, 2025), p. 203.

order of battle, allowing units to move into square more quickly, given the numbers of Ottoman cavalry they would face. Suvorov would adopt the idea of speed because it created the possibility of surprise: 'Money is dear; human life is still dearer; but time is the dearest of all.'

This was set out in Rumyantsev's general ordinance (*Rite of Service*) after he took command of the First Army in 1770. More training was to be undertaken in the regiment rather than in regional training battalions. A two-rank firing line was preferred to maximise firepower. The cavalry would also charge in two ranks at full gallop, with the cuirassiers giving up their cuirasses to increase speed. Most significantly, the army would fight in multiple divisional squares rather than the whole army square. Cavalry would operate between the squares and on the flanks. Grenadiers and jägers would lead the attack and provide the face of the square in defence.

Duffy argues that Rumyantsev was 'probably the most important single formative influence on the Russian army in the second half of the eighteenth century.'[9] It was Suvorov who would take forward his ideas and later exclaim, 'Suvorov is the pupil of Rumyantsev.' Staff work improved, infantry and artillery fought well against much larger Ottoman forces, and the development of light troops was vital in such a vast theatre of war. The value of training was also emphasised. In Suvorov's words, 'Training meant "light," while lack of training spelt "darkness."'[10]

The value of light and irregular troops had been recognised by all European armies during the Seven Years' War, with even Prussian regulars adapting to them with tactics like hedge-firing, a form of controlled skirmishing by volleys. However, light troops rarely played a significant role on the battlefield; their strength lay in the war of outposts, convoy attacks, and seizing objectives ahead of the main army. Austria and Russia had more experience with this form of warfare due to their wars against the Ottomans and the frequent border conflicts that occurred between wars.

Post-war reforms

Following the 1768 war, the army was reformed and expanded under Grigory Potemkin's direction, in line with the new focus on expansion to the south. Potemkin was the effective army chief from 1774 and was formally appointed Field Marshal and President of the Council in 1784. Between 1767 and 1786, the

---

9. C. Duffy, *Russia's Military Way to the West*, (Routledge, 1981), p.173.

10. B. Menning, *Train Hard, Fight Easy: The Legacy of A.V. Suvorov and his 'Art of Victory'*, (Air University Review, Dec. 1986), p. 79.

infantry expanded by 75,000 and the cavalry by 30,000, bringing the total strength to 230,000 infantry and 62,000 regular cavalry. The recruiting levy remained stable, with the increase primarily resulting from the growing populations of the new territories. He notably increased the light cavalry and jägers, vital to the vast space he had to operate in. There was a 4,000-strong Jäger Corps, commanded by Kutuzov on the Bug River between 1786 and 1788. Kutuzov published a military treatise, *Remarks on Infantry Service in General, and That of the Jägers in Particular*. Unlike similar works, this was, for Russia, a subject that had not been considered before, and demonstrated original thinking. He proposed lighter uniforms, shorter rifles and target practice to ensure accurate fire. His views on the welfare of his troops matched Potemkin's, who noted that there was not a single case of desertion in the Bug Jäger Corps.[11] Jäger battalions were later issued with two battalion guns like the line regiments, which necessitated further training in coordination.

Potemkin created new regiments of grenadiers from peasants in former monastic estates, calling again on Kutuzov to train them, and these units would play a vital role in the 1787 war. There were also some exotic new units, including Potemkin's short-lived Israelovsky unit, which was a mixed Jewish infantry and cavalry unit, all the more remarkable given Russian and, particularly, Cossack anti-Semitism. The artillery retained the earlier reforms, although lighter guns were introduced in 1788. The army was still organised in divisions, which was consistent with the doctrine of squares and attack columns. Field battalions were formed on the Ukrainian Line for local defence, and Cossack infantry remained in the garrisons at Azov and Kerch. Cuirassiers lost their breastplates and became almost indistinguishable tactically from the carabiniers, who now made up a larger proportion of the cavalry. Cavalry was organised into squadrons instead of companies. There were also ten new dragoon regiments by 1783, along with squadrons of mounted jägers and grenadiers.

While the official doctrine remained unchanged, in practice, the army in the south adopted Potemkin's training principles, with its emphasis on the offensive. Preference was given to smaller regimental and battalion squares rather than the old divisional versions. Potemkin also introduced his own uniform changes, describing the existing uniforms as 'ideally suited to the torment of our soldiers.' These included a shorter, looser coat and trousers, eliminating gaiters, buckles and powdered hair and pigtails, which had taken two hours to prepare each day. The tricorn was replaced by the Potemkin helmet, with a peaked felt casque with a wool cross-roll to better protect the head and neck from the rain and sun.

---

11. A. Mikaberidze, *Kutuzov: A Life in War and Peace*, (Oxford, 2022), p. 52.

Potemkin uniforms (Knotel)

Duffy highlights the scale of the Russian military by looking at the demands on industry. Pig and cast iron production increased from 15,000 tons in Peter the Great's reign to 160,000 tons at the end of the century. There were fifteen artillery factories and small arms factories, although the quality of Russian muskets remained poor. An English visitor commented, 'Their firearms are very bad, and one thousand men are never exercised without two or three bursting, and killing or wounding some of their men.'[12] It was perhaps unsurprising that Suvorov prioritised the bayonet: 'If three Turks attack a Russian in battle, he was to bayonet the first, shoot the second and bayonet the third.' The supply system was also riddled with corruption and inefficiency. Potemkin, for all his many talents, was not a competent administrator. Russian staff work was also not at the same standard as that of the French and Austrians.

A mixed evaluation of the army emerged from the 1787–92 war. The infantry, with their new practical uniforms, performed well, particularly the grenadiers. However, the cavalry was less well regarded, and excessive baggage was still a hindrance to manoeuvre. Western observers were critical of the Russian army's lack of professionalism and disregard for military science, citing its poor performance during the period. Catherine dismissed these criticisms, pointing to results her generals had achieved: 'All the battles they have won, all the towns they have taken, the variety of European and Asiatic troops they have beaten, and the multitude of provinces they have conquered.' It cannot be denied that the army won both wars and was a bastion of state power, illustrated by its suppression of the Pugachev rebellion. The Russian military was effective, if not efficient.

---

12. C. Duffy, *Russia's Military Way to the West*, (Routledge, 1981), p. 179.

Austrian Army

In the 1787 war, Russia was allied with Austria, which sent significant forces into Moldavia to fight alongside Suvorov. Space precludes a detailed examination of the Austrian army, which is covered in Christopher Duffy's books on the subject.

The Austrian army's experience in the Balkans deteriorated after Prince Eugene's great victories against the Ottomans, which culminated in the capture of Belgrade during the 1716–18 campaign. He had died when they lost Belgrade and the war against the Ottomans in 1737–39. The Austrian army had performed reasonably well during the Seven Years' War, taking on and often beating the Prussian army that was reckoned to be the finest in the world. However, the cost was massive, with a loss of 303,594 men over six years of campaigning.[13]

The army in our period was led by generals who had made their names during the Seven Years' War, with Emperor Joseph II playing a greater role as co-regent with Maria Theresa after 1765. He presented a paper calling for a larger army based on the Prussian cantonal system of conscription, although the Chancellor Kaunitz argued that it was unaffordable. The compromise was an army of 200,000, which attracted favourable attention, even from Frederick the Great.

Field Marshal Lacy led the post-war army. He opposed the First Partition of Poland, arguing that the open country and Polish population added nothing to the empire. During the Bavarian Succession Crisis (1778–9), his plan to defend Bohemia frustrated the Prussian advance. After inconclusive mountain skirmishes in the winter, a peace deal was reached in May 1779.

The 1781 alliance with the Russians obliged the Austrians to join the war against the Ottomans in 1788, although the Austrians were distracted by unrest in Belgium. They still managed to deploy six armies to cover the lengthy border with the Ottomans, mobilising 245,000 men and 898 field guns. However, Austrian doctrine did not adapt well to warfare against the Ottomans, relying on large squares at a time when the Russians were adopting more flexible formations. This led to a defensive doctrine, and the cavalry returned to wearing helmets and cuirasses. The exception was the light troops, Croats from the military border. As author M. Hochedlinger concludes, 'Austria's rather bureaucratic way of waging war, very much concerned with preserving men and material, could not compete with the Russian variety of warfare merging modern western military organisation with atavistic traits of "Asi-

---

13. C. Duffy, *The Army of Maria Theresa*, (Terence Wise, 1990), p. 205.

atic" ruthlessness (both against one's own men and the enemy) which repeatedly shocked Europe.'[14]

The Commanders

Count Pyotr Alexandrovich Rumyantsev-Zadunaisky (1725–1796)

Rumyantsev was one of Russia's greatest military commanders, although he is less well known in the West than his eighteenth-century contemporaries, Suvorov and Potemkin. He was the commander of the main Russian army at the outset of the war. He was born into a Russian noble family; his father, Count Alexander Rumyantsev, was a diplomat and one of Peter the Great's aides. The family was so close to Peter the Great that it was rumoured that he was the illegitimate son of the Emperor, after whom he was named and who became his godfather. He may have been born in modern-day Moldova; his father was the governor of Little Russia (modern-day Ukraine), although other sources claim it was Moscow.

Pyotr Rumyantsev in the 1770s

He served in various military campaigns early in his career, including the Russo-Swedish War (1741–1743), during which he was promoted to the rank of colonel. During the War of the Austrian Succession (1740–48), he commanded forces on the Dniester River, gaining valuable knowledge of European military practices. In the Seven Years' War (1756–63), he commanded a division at the Battle of Gross-Jägersdorf (1757) and captured Kolberg after a siege in 1761, cutting Prussia off from its supplies via the Baltic. During this conflict, he introduced innovative tactics such as columns and jägers into Russian military doctrine, along with flexibility and coordination between infantry, cavalry, and artillery. He wrote the *Instructions* (1761), the first of several military works, which were taken up in later reforms.

He was appointed Governor of Little Russia in 1764, which put him at the seat of war in 1768. He commanded the army sent to capture Azov, defeating the Ottomans in the battles of Larga and Kagul. He then crossed the Danube and advanced into modern-day Bulgaria, achievements that resulted in his promotion to Field Marshal and the title Zadunaisky ('Trans-Danubian'). It was Rumyanstev who signed the armistice at Küçük Kaynarca in 1774. He returned to successive governor roles until he died in 1796.

Prince Vasily Mikhailovich Dolgorukov-Krymsky (1722–1782)

Dolgorukov

Dolgorukov was the commander of the 2nd Field Army during the 1768 war, initially tasked with sealing off the Crimea, and later invading the Tatar Khanate. He was born in 1722 into a princely family, although his uncle was accused of plotting and insulting Empress Anna in 1731, thereby bringing disgrace upon the entire family. Dolgorukov joined the army at the age of thirteen as a private because the Empress had banned any of his family members from holding officer positions. He distinguished himself at the Siege of Perekop in the Crimea under Munnich, who persuaded the Empress to relent. Under Elizabeth, he was rapidly promoted, reaching the rank of colonel by 1747.

He was a major-general during the Seven Years' War, fighting at the Siege of Küstrin and the Battle of Zorndorf in August 1758. Promoted for valour to lieutenant-general, he was wounded later in the campaign but recovered in time to lead an infantry brigade at the Battle of Kunersdorf in August 1759. He served under Rumyanstev at the Siege of Kolberg. Catherine awarded him the Order of St. Andrew, the highest order of knighthood in the Russian Empire, in 1767.

During the 1768 war, he sealed off the Crimea, stopping the Tatars from attacking the rear of Rumyanstev's army. In 1771, he captured Perekop and invaded the Crimea, defeating the Tatars at the Battle of Kefe (Feodosia) in July. This led to the Russians conquering Crimea and installing a puppet ruler. At the peace, he was awarded the addition of *Krymsky* ('of Crimea') to the family name, but retired to his estates after he wasn't granted the rank of field marshal.

Count Alexei Grigoryevich Orlov-Chesmensky (1737–1808)

Orlov was born into a noble family, the son of the governor of Novgorod, in 1737. He entered the Preobrazhensky Guards Regiment and by 1762 had reached the rank of sergeant, fighting in the Seven Years' War. He was over two meters tall, a celebrated duellist, and had a scar across his cheek, which earned him the nickname 'Scarface.'

Alexei Orlov

He rose to power through his involvement in the palace coup (with his brother Grigory, who was Catherine's lover) that led to Catherine gaining the throne, probably murdering Tsar Peter III. He was rewarded with the rank of major-general, the title of count, and large estates. He was interested in new ideas, corresponding with Rousseau; and he helped found the learned Free Economic Society. His agricultural interests have left a legacy in the form of the Orlov Trotter horse breed, and a breed of chicken still known as the Orloff.

At the outset of the 1768 war, he was promoted to the rank of general-admiral and commanded the fleet during the First Archipelago Exhibition, which led to the Orlov Revolt in the Peloponnese. He defeated an Ottoman fleet at the Battle of Chesme on 5 July 1770, and was awarded the honorific 'Chesmensky' to his name. He sought overall command of the armed forces in the 1787 war and refused Catherine's offer of the Black Sea Fleet, refusing to serve under Potemkin. After the war, the Orlovs fell from favour, and he left the country after Catherine's death. He returned when Alexander I gained the throne and commanded militia forces during the Napoleonic Wars, passing away in 1808.

Samuel Greig (1735–1788)

Samuel Greig was born in Inverkeithing, Fife, in 1735. He worked on his father's ships before joining the Royal Navy in 1758 as a master's mate. He fought the battles of Quiberon Bay (1759) and Havana (1762) and was promoted to lieutenant. He was sent to Russia as one of a team of naval officers to help improve the Russian Navy, and was promoted to captain. One of many Scots who fought in European wars.

Samuel Greig in 1772

In 1770, he was part of Orlov's Mediterranean fleet, and was promoted to commodore before the Battle of Chesme while in command of the fire ships. In an outstanding feat of bravery, he personally set the match to the fire ships and then swam to his own boats under fire. In recognition of this feat, he was promoted to admiral.

He continued to reform the Russian Navy, and after the war was promoted to the rank of Admiral of the Russian Empire. He died of a fever on board his ship during the Battle of Hogland (1788) during the Russo-Swedish War and was buried in Tallinn. His family continued his service in the Russian Navy, with his son Alexey also reaching the rank of admiral.

Count Ivan Petrovich Saltykov (1797–1804)

Ivan Saltykov

Ivan Saltykov was the son of Field-Marshal Pyotr Saltykov, the author of the army reforms outlined above. He began military service at the age of fifteen in the Semenovsky Regiment. During the Seven Years' War, he distinguished himself in the capture of both Königsberg and Elbing, as well as at the Battle of Zorndorf. After the war, he was promoted to major general.

Before the war, he was promoted to Lieutenant-General and served under the command of Rumyantsev at the Battle of Kagul (1770). He also fought in the capture of the fortress at Khotyn. As the commander of the army's heavy cavalry, he gained several distinctions for his bravery, although others criticised his tactical skills. After the war, he was promoted to full general and concluded his service as a General Field Marshal, serving as Viceroy of the Caucasus and Governor-General of Moscow. He retired in 1804 and died shortly afterwards.

Count Alexander Vasilyevich Suvorov-Rymniksky (1730–1800)

Suvorov is one of Russia's most famous commanders, and arguably the finest, who came to prominence during this period. However, he is probably better known for his commands during the French Revolutionary Wars. He was born into a noble family in Moscow in 1730 and joined the army at the age of seventeen. He was promoted to Colonel of the Suzdal Regiment after his actions in the Seven Years' War. He wrote a novel training manual that emphasised realistic war manoeuvres over Prussian-style drill.

Alexander Suvorov by Steuben

In the War of the Bar Confederation (1768–1772), he successfully led Russian forces in a series of engagements against the Polish confederates, using rapid marches and unorthodox tactics to outmanoeuvre their troops. At the Battle of Lanckorona (1771) he defeated the Bar Confederates, despite their strong defensive position, by a pincer movement. He went on to capture Kraków (1772), leading to the collapse of the Confederation and the First Partition of Poland in 1772. He then shifted to the main seat of the war against the Ottomans and was nearly captured at the siege of Turtukaya in 1773. As a Lieutenant-General, he won, with Kamensky, the Battle of Kozludzha (1774), cementing his reputation.

Suvorov was promoted to general after the war and commanded Russian forces in the subsequent Ottoman War (1787–92), winning victories at Rymnik and Focşani, as well as the siege of Izmail. Rapid marching was a key feature of his strategy. He was a great believer in training and exercising his troops, saying, 'Train hard, fight easy. Train easy, and you will have hard fighting.' His *Art of Victory* was published in 1795, stressing the importance of *coup d'oeil* (swift decisions), speed, and impact. His emphasis on the bayonet was probably more relevant in siege storming when firing could result in a loss of impetus. Noted for his eccentricity, he was better educated and more knowledgeable than he was portrayed in the Western media, and the welfare of his troops was a high priority.

He later put down the Polish Uprising (1794), and after falling out with Paul I, was recalled to lead Russian forces in the French Revolutionary Wars. Suvorov died in 1800 in Saint Petersburg.

Prince Mikhail Illarionovich Golenishchev-Kutuzov-Smolensky (1745–1813)

Kutuzov is another Russian commander during these wars who is better known for his service during later conflicts, particularly the 1812 campaign. He was born into a military family, with his father serving in the engineers. He followed his father's service by enrolling in the military engineering school and later teaching there.

In 1762, Kutuzov was a captain in the Astrakhan Infantry Regiment, commanded by Colonel Alexander Suvorov. He learned much from Suvorov, including the importance of clear orders, proper training, and taking care of his soldiers' health. He developed his battlefield skills in the War of the Bar Confederation (1768–1772), before joining Rumyantsev's army for the campaign against the Ottomans. His campaign received a setback when an officer reported to Rumyantsev that Kutuzov mocked him behind his back. Rumyantsev had the then-Lieutenant-Colonel Kutuzov transferred to Dolgorukov's Second Army, which was fighting the Tatars in the Crimea. He was seriously wounded in the left eye while leading the attack on Alushta. This was almost certainly a fatal wound in this period, but Kutuzov gradually recovered.

Kutuzov in 1777

He travelled extensively after the war and became known for the breadth of his military knowledge, with a particular focus on Jäger tactics. He fought in the 1787 Russo-Ottoman War as a major-general, distinguishing himself at Izmail and Macin. Later, he served as a diplomat in Constantinople. He commanded the Russian army at Austerlitz, although the Tsar ignored his advice. He was recalled to lead the campaigns against the Ottomans in the Balkans before defeating Napoleon in 1812. He died in 1813.

Prince Grigory Aleksandrovich Potemkin-Tauricheski (1739–1791)

Potemkin is closely associated with Russian colonial expansion in the south, his service as the later governor of the southern provinces, and his major building projects on the Black Sea coast. He made his military reputation in the 1768 war.

He was born into a modest noble landowning family near Smolensk. He attended Moscow University and enlisted in the army, later joining the Horse Guards. He participated in the palace coup that brought Catherine to power and was promoted to second lieutenant, then was appointed *Kammerjunker* (gentleman of the bedchamber)—a fitting role, as he later became Catherine's lover.

After several diplomatic posts, he pleaded with Catherine to be allowed to serve in the 1768 war: 'The only way I can express my gratitude to Your Majesty is to shed my blood for Your glory.'[15] Potemkin served as Major-General of the cavalry. He fought in the Khotyn campaign at Kamenets, and in August excelled at the Battle of Prashkovsky, leading to praise by his commander Golitsyn: 'Our cavalry has never acted with such discipline and courage as it did under the command of the Major-General.' Under Rumyantsev, he received further awards for bravery, and returned to St. Petersburg in 1772 as a war hero, although he had to recover from illness.

Potemkin aged 35

After the war, he was appointed Adjutant General and became Catherine's lover, probably marrying her in secret in 1774. The British ambassador recognised Potemkin as the coming man, writing, 'Given these qualities, and thanks to the indolence of his rivals, he ought naturally to hope that he can elevate himself to the heights envisioned by his boundless ambitions.' He held many appointments even after separating from Catherine, most significantly as Governor-General of Novorossiya (New Russia), where he expanded the territory and built ports and towns, including Kherson, Nikolayev, Sevastopol, and Ekaterinoslav (modern Dnipro). Potemkin was the effective head of the War College from 1774, driving military reforms that formed the basis of the Russian army that fought again in 1787. He died of bronchial pneumonia in 1791, while preparing for a further war in the south.

Prince Alexander Mikhailovich Golitsyn (1718–1783)

Golitsyn commanded the main army until Rumyantsev replaced him after the Battle of Khotyn. Born into a princely family in 1718, he started a military career. However, the family was out of favour with Empress Anna, so he spent seventeen years in the Austrian army. Back in favour under Elizabeth, he rose to the rank of lieutenant general and commanded the Russian left flank at Kunersdorf during the Seven Years' War.

On Catherine's accession, he joined the High Court Council and was appointed to command the main army advancing on Khotyn. However, he was outnumbered, and withdrew to draw the Ottoman forces onto more favourable ground. Catherine decided to replace him with Rumyantsev, but before he arrived, Golitsyn defeated the Ottomans and then captured Khotyn. He was made a field marshal as compensation for being relieved. After the war, he continued in high office, including as governor general of Saint Petersburg. He died in 1783.

Chapter Seven

The Ottoman Army

Introduction

As we have seen, the Ottoman army in the eighteenth century, while past its prime, was still capable of defeating its enemies. The Russians in the Prut campaign, the Venetians in the Morea, and the Austrians in 1736–39 had all faced an army that was able to mobilise and supply large numbers of troops and achieve victory on the battlefield. The military remained the core of the ruling elite, with few distinctions between civilian and military roles, and Turks viewed the army as a highly desirable career path. Western sources have tended to emphasise the weaknesses of their opponents rather than Ottoman resilience, the competence of commanders, and the valour exercised by the troops.

The weaknesses that became apparent in the coming war were not a surprise to everyone in the Ottoman establishment. Ibrahim Müteferrika, in his 1732 reform treatise, cited Peter the Great's reforms as being based on imitating victorious nations.[1] He emphasised the importance of maintaining balanced troop proportions, employing military experts, providing superior training, and instilling discipline through drilling. The Ottomans had also learned from their enemies and had been early adopters of firepower and logistics. Foreign experts were also employed, including engineers and artillerymen, such as the Frenchman Comte de Bonneval. The *Tayfa-i Efrenciye* (Corps of Europeans) was a recognised part of the army.

However, a long period of peace had led to complacency, and reforms were rarely sustained as those favouring reform clashed with conservatives who wanted to return to the 'uncorrupted' state. The Ottoman military system had not developed either an officer class or the disciplined infantry or artillery which were the bedrock

---

1. V. Aksan, *Ottoman Wars 1700–1870*, (Pearson, 2007), p.118.

of their opponents. The decline in military discipline, particularly among the Kapikulu Corps, along with the weakening of the *sipahis'* effectiveness, eroded the traditional strengths of the Ottoman army. The army that would face the Russians was based on the Kapikulu, primarily consisting of the Janissaries, and a smaller force of regular cavalry. Non-Kapikulu troops were called by a bewildering variety of names, typically grouped under the titles *serhaddkulu* or *levend* by our period. The use of peasants as soldiers broke the traditional demarcation line between peasant and soldier, which would have long-term implications for the Ottoman state.

In terms of military administration, while the Russians were centralising, the Ottomans decentralised, with provincial forces becoming increasingly important. The grand vizier was still the commander-in-chief, but the old Ottoman practice of assembling the army near Constantinople and marching to the front had been replaced by a more decentralised system. This increased its dependence on the provincial elites and provincial military forces. In 1761–62, Ottoman central troops numbered 55,731 men, with an additional 141,116 men in the garrisons. Of the latter, 55,721 were Janissaries, armourers, and artillerists, serving in the empire's forts. The remaining 85,395 were local infantry and cavalry garrison troops.[2] With many Janissaries in Istanbul unfit for mobilisation, garrisons had to be maintained outside the war zone. Exact numbers and Ottoman troop dispositions are always challenging, but some records do exist.[3]

As Virginia Aksan, a foremost scholar of the Ottoman Empire, puts it, 'The empire, in fact, was relying in peace time on an army, salaried but ill-paid, ill-educated and ill-trained, whose complicated relationship with Istanbul and provincial societies, as both state representatives and local grandees, made them an extremely unreliable force.'[4]

The Janissaries

The Janissaries were founded in the fourteenth century as an elite corps recruited through the *devşirme* system of child levies, by which European Christian boys (usually between ten and twenty years old), mainly from the Balkans, were taken, forced to convert to Islam, and incorporated into the Ottoman army. Many rose to

---

2. G. Agostan, *Military Transformation in the Ottoman Empire and Russia, 1500–1800*, (Kritika: Explorations in Russia and Eurasian History, 12:2, spring 2011), p. 303.

3. V. Velikanov, *Ottoman Army's Strength and Organization at the at the beginning of the Russo-Turkish War of 1768–1774*, (Academic Publishing House, 2018).

4. V. Aksan, *An Ottoman Statesman in War and Peace: Ahmed Resmi Efendi, 1700–1783*, (Brill, 1995), p. 14.

senior positions in the Ottoman establishment, and some families willingly offered their sons because of the prospects of advancement. The *devşirme* was abolished in 1648, and the children of Janissaries were allowed to enrol. along with other civilians. Recruits were more likely to come from western and northern Anatolia than the Balkans. The elite fighting corps, the backbone of early Ottoman victories, started to lose its military character and incorporated civilian trades. They could, and did, mutiny and hinder reforms to the army structure, even changing the sultans through palace coups. They rioted in Istanbul during peacetime, sometimes fighting among themselves as well as terrorising civilians. The British ambassador reported on fighting between Janissaries in Galata, which went on for days: 'The houses and shops were all shut up; no one durst venture into the streets.'[5] In contrast, the Janissaries also served as a police force in the capital and other cities, enforcing fair trade—a rare uniformed presence on the streets in a period that generally preceded the establishment of police forces.

Agha of the Janissaries

Janissaries were organised into *ortas* (regiments) whose strengths varied considerably, with some having specific functions. There were 161 combat *orta* in the 1760s, and another 34 in non-combat roles. Janissaries were paid monthly (in theory), lived in barracks, and were promoted based on length of service or favouritism. Initially based in Constantinople, by our period they were dispersed around the Empire in garrisons. These Janissaries put down roots and became part of the local leadership, known as *yerliyyas*. Each *orta* could be identified by an emblem on their flag and equipment, and was commanded by a *çorbaci*, which means 'the ones who supply the soup,' reflecting the special privilege of receiving food from someone who represents the Sultan. There were five officers, with varying names depending on their history, but typically including an assistant commander, quartermaster, standard bearer, and assistant standard bearer. The Agha of the Janissaries commanded the Janissary corps. They used a heavier flintlock musket that was slower to reload but had a longer range than Western muskets. They retained the sword and objected to the bayonet. This reflected individual initiative rather than what they viewed as the mindless automatons they faced in Western armies. However, in practice, they had

---

5. The National Archives: FO SP97/48, *Sir John Murray to Foreign Office.* (3 March 1772)

partially lost their discipline, and resistance to innovation weakened their effectiveness on the battlefield. Training was limited to weapon skills rather than drill and tactics.

There are conflicting estimates of the number of Janissaries in 1768, ranging from 60,000 to some 400,000 pay coupons in circulation. The fighting force was probably in the 30,000–40,000 range, with 20,000–30,000 (more later in the war) reaching the front. We don't know much about their tactics. They are shown as deploying in columns and fighting in deep formations (9–12 ranks) to allow continuous fire by rotating rows forward. There are some references to skirmishing, although this may have been more common after the 1768 war. After the firefight, Janissaries would draw their swords and charge en masse, fighting individually. Flaherty and others compare this tactic to the Highland charge, although the Janissaries could engage in a longer fire-fight than the Highlanders.

Levend and local troops

There are many different names associated with Ottoman provincial troops of the period, such as *Azab*, *Seğban*, *Tüfenkci*, *Yamak*, *Serica*, *Arnaut*, and others. The *levend*, the locally mustered soldier, had become central to the Ottoman wartime military by 1750. Recruited in a standardised format by a combination of state-appointed and locally appointed officials, they formed the core of the Ottoman army in the 1768 war. Aksan references registers and account books that show as many as 100,000–150,000 of these troops reaching the front, although death and desertion rates could be as high as one in two.[6]

Orders for levend troops were sent to the governors of *sancaks* (who often commanded their troops) with details of the numbers (companies of fifty) to be sent, sign-up bonus (double for cavalry), pay, and rations. There was also money for equipment, which could sometimes be provided from central stores, although troops may have been expected to bring their own small arms and cavalrymen a horse. A six-month period of service was standard, but this could be extended if required to allow for the journey to the front and winter quarters. Some families became wealthy and powerful as contractors of levend troops, as did the *ayans* who contributed large numbers of such forces. Officers (*ondalik*) received a 10 per cent commission. Recruits were expected to 'be upright, handsome Muslims, committed to war for the faith.' In practice, they may have fallen somewhat short of this standard. As one commander commented,

---

6. V. Aksan, *Whatever Happened to the Janissaries? Mobilization for the 1768–1774 Russo-Ottoman War*, (War in History, Vol. 5, No. 1, January 1998), p. 29.

'The paşas from Anatolia recruited thieves and the homeless and then were held captive by them — at every hamlet or bridge-crossing, the men demanded salaries and bonuses, a tyranny completely contrary to custom. Such men were disruptive in camp, by his estimation. Even though the paşas brought along enough men for a battalion, in three days they had scattered, and they could not even raise 100 men.'[7]

This level of indiscipline could lead to mutiny, as happened among the *yamaks* (fortress guards) in the Khotyn fortress in May 1769.[8] Despite these challenges, commanders acknowledged that there was no shortage of troops, with some complaining that they had too many. The personal guards of the provincial governors would have been more disciplined. They were maintained at the expense of the governor, described as *yeri kulu* (local slaves), and could serve in both infantry and cavalry roles. Originally recruited for garrison duties, they gradually became involved in campaigns outside their region. The levend infantry were typically armed with a musket and a hand weapons (typically a long knife called a *yataghan*), and fought as firepower infantry. There are also references to the *Dalkalichi* (sword drawing), volunteer fanatical Muslims who regarded war with the Russians as a jihad. They are noted by the Russians as attacking with sabres, singing *surahs* from the Koran.[9]

Albanian Irregular (New York Public Library Digital Collections.)

The levend infantryman rations consisted of 320 gm of bread, 160 gm of biscuit, and 641 gm of meat, which was similar to Janissary rations. The cavalryman was entitled to the same amount of bread, but only 320 gm of meat, plus 320 gm of rice, 80 gm of cooking oil, and 6.5 kg of barley. This was significantly more than the rations of a Russian soldier who relied heavily on foraging. Ottoman troops expected their rations in kind, although cash substitution was common, particularly for the levend. How far any of these ration amounts were achieved in wartime is

---

7. V. Aksan, *Whatever Happened to the Janissaries? Mobilization for the 1768–1774 Russo-Ottoman War*, (War in History, Vol. 5, No. 1, January 1998), p. 34.

8. V. Aksan, *Mutiny and the Eighteenth Century Ottoman Army*, (Turkish Studies Association Bulletin, Vol. 22, No. 1, Spring 1998), pp. 116–125.

9. V. Velikanov, *Ottoman Army's Strength and Organization at the beginning of the Russo-Turkish War of 1768–1774*, (Academic Publishing House, 2018), p. 138.

unclear, although the few individual stories we have complain that the cash rarely paid for the stated rations.

The levend troops fought side by side with the Janissaries in the field and fortresses. They were a pragmatic response to the need to get more soldiers to the front than the Janissaries could provide. It was also a response to the increasing cost of warfare that would have implications for the Ottoman state. The recruitment of so many local troops must also have had an impact on the local economy. In peacetime, they often resorted to brigandage due to the absence of alternative employment. Albanian soldiers acted as bandits during peacetime and irregulars during wartime, frequently serving right across the empire.

Cavalry

The traditional Ottoman cavalryman was the *sipahi*, based on the *timar*, a land grant in return for military service of himself and retainers (*jebelu*), depending on the size of the *timar*. It was not precisely analogous to the feudal system, as there was no guarantee that the timar would be passed down to descendants, although it was usually done. They also had the feudal weakness of needing to return to their land in winter to collect the revenues required to sustain themselves in the field. By this period, the timar system had declined. The revenues did not support the obligations, and many were struck off as the sipahi failed to turn up, and even those who did were often ill-equipped. Other timars were converted into tax farms, and the state used these revenues to pay for an increasing proportion of infantry in Ottoman armies. Ottoman records do not include *timariots* in 1768, although observers reference the type, in small numbers. By this period, sipahis were lightly equipped, typically with a lance (although the sword was emphasised more in the eighteenth century), pistols, and a musket or bow. Some may have operated like dragoons.[10]

The Kapikulu cavalry (sometimes referred to as Sipahi of the Porte or *suvarileri*) were the mounted counterparts of the Janissaries, traditionally based in Constantinople but increasingly serving in the provinces. The commander had the title of *sipahilar ağasi*, and it was organised into two divisions. With the growth in infantry, their role was diminished, but there were still around 12,000 in this period, even if the fighting element of the corps was probably no more than 3,000. The elite regiments could be heavily armoured, wearing full body suits of Indian or Persian chain mail armour, some with breastplates but not the full cuirass of Western armies. Individuals were typically armed with a spear, bow, sabre, pistols and mace.

---

10. C. Flaherty, *The Napoleonic Ottoman Army*, (Partizan Press, 2019), p. 65 and p. 72.

Sipahi (New York Public Library Digital Collections.)

Provincial cavalry included paid volunteers known as *deli* (*delhi, deliher*), which in Turkish means 'mad-head,' due to their courage. Initially frontier cavalry raised from recent converts to Islam, their motto was 'only God determined the end of one's life.' In this period, they were typically the personal guard units of provincial governors in the Balkans, formed in companies of fifty to sixty men commanded by a *delibasi*. They were disciplined light cavalry (unlike the levend units) who would be very prepared to charge in battle.

The traditional light cavalry roles in the vanguard of the army were usually performed by Tatars, primarily based in Crimea. However, other tribes were settled in the Balkans (mainly Dobruja) and the North Caucasus (Circassia). Around 26,000 were available for deployment in 1786. They were armed with a cavalry spear, a sword, and a bow. Tactics were traditional nomad methods based on massed volleys of arrows as large numbers swarmed around the enemy. Feigned retreats and flanking attacks were also deployed. Baron de Tott, the French consul to Crimea in 1767, described Tatar horsemen on campaign as carrying a bag containing six pounds of millet flour, which lasted them thirty days. 'He mounts his horse, stops not until the sun goes down, then clogs the animal, leaves him to graze, sups on his flour, goes to sleep, awakes and continues his route. It is certainly to be feared that a people, so patient, may, one day, furnish formidable armies.'[11]

---

11. F. De Tott, *Memoirs of Baron de Tott*, (Vol. 1, G & J Robinson, London, 1785), p. 49.

Tactically, Ottoman cavalry typically operated on the flanks, protecting the infantry, which did not form a square formation. They aimed to use their superior numbers to outflank an enemy and were trained to operate in rough terrain. This was possible due to the loose formations they adopted, manoeuvring as individuals rather than in formation. Western observers had a high opinion of Ottoman cavalry, compared to their own. However, disciplined infantry, which were typically formed in squares (as the Russians often did) could usually defeat their attacks.

Artillery and Engineers

Tatar (New York Public Library Digital Collections.)

The artillery troops were organised in a similar way to the Janissaries, and formed their corps of the *kapikulu* in Constantinople. During our period, they were also dispersed throughout the empire, similar to the Janissaries. They produced the guns in the Tophane foundry, and maintained and served them on campaign. They were also responsible for the army reserves of gunpowder, carts, and carriages. Powder was produced in factories across the empire, although the demands of war meant substantial quantities were imported from Europe. The artillery had been reformed with the assistance of a French officer, Claude de Bonneval, in the 1730s. As a technical corps with less political and economic power, they were less likely to resist change, but his reforms still declined when he left.

Ottoman field gun ((New York Public Library Digital Collections.)

The traditional Ottoman artillery (topijis) was based on field guns (kolunburna), light guns (darbzen), and siege guns (basilisks). The field guns were primarily single-piece, cast bronze barrels of varying weights, ranging up to 9 kg. Light guns of up to 2.5 kg would be deployed with the infantry and could be mounted on wagons. The siege guns and fortress artillery could range up to 17 kg, and included stone-firing cannons. Field guns were often formed into position batteries used to bombard the enemy before an infantry attack, although their rate of fire was lower than that of their Russian opponents.

The *Lağimici Ocaği* (mine layers) were the traditional engineers of the army. The miners operated as pioneers (as well as mining during sieges) and could be drawn from non-Muslim populations. They worked closely with the *Humbaraci Ocaği* (mortar corps), who specialised in siege warfare and were recruited mainly from Bosnia. They deployed a variety of mortars, ranging from massive pieces that fired stone balls (104–246 kg) to smaller weapons that fired balls weighing 17–55 kg. By 1771–72, only three types weighing 18, 23, and 41 kg were cast at Tophane.[12] The numbers are unclear, but they probably totalled around 20,000.

In the wars of the late eighteenth century, the Ottomans extensively utilised field fortifications, often in the form of multiple trenches supported by artillery positioned on *gabions* (round baskets filled with earth and stones) or earth bags. The Austrian Field Marshal Laudon complimented Ottoman engineering and fortress defence, saying, 'It is beyond all human powers of comprehension to grasp how strongly these places are built, and just how obstinately the Turks defend them.'[13] Others were less impressed. De Tott, visiting Ochakov and Kinburn, noted how the artillery was poorly sited, allowing ships to sail down the middle of the estuary. Ottoman artillery was moved by rope harness rather than limbers, which, along with size, made them difficult to manoeuvre. Russian commanders observed, 'Both the carriages under them with such inconvenience, and their gunners with such inexperience, that they do not have the ability to quickly aim their guns at the enemy, nor even turn them from side to side, which is why their guns…firing for

---

12. B. Mugnai, *The Ottoman Army of the Napoleonic Wars*, (Helion, 2022), p. 115.

13. M. Mayer, *Joseph II and the Austro-Ottoman war, 1788–1791*, (University of Cambridge Repository, 2002), p. 88–89

the most part all at the one place where they first begin, very little, or so to speak, almost no harm to the enemy.'[14]

Commanders

Sultan Mustafa III (1717–1774)

Mustafa III was the sultan of the Ottoman Empire from 1757 to 1774. He was born at the Edirne Palace on 28 January 1717, the son of Sultan Ahmed III. In 1730, after the Patrona Halil revolt led to his father's deposition, Mustafa, his father, and his brothers were imprisoned in the Topkapı Palace. In 1757, after the death of his cousin Osman III, he ascended the throne.

An admirer of Frederick the Great, he agreed to a peace treaty with Prussia in 1761, exchanged diplomats, and recruited Prussian military advisors. Successive grand viziers supported a peace policy, but the increasing influence of Russia over the Caucasus and Poland created tension between the Ottomans and Russia. Mustafa overruled Grand Vizier Muhsinzade Mehmed Pasha, expecting an easy victory, although his armed forces were unprepared for war after a long period of peace. Mustafa died of a heart attack on 21 January 1774 at the Topkapı Palace. He was buried in his mausoleum at Laleli Mosque in Istanbul. His brother Abdul Hamid I succeeded him.

Sultan Abdul Hamid I (1774-1789)

Abdul Hamid was born on 20 March 1725 in Constantinople. He was a younger son of Sultan Ahmed III and brother of Mustafa III. He spent most of the fifty years preceding his ascension to the throne in 1774 in the seclusion of the palace, focusing on religious affairs.

Abdul Hamid I (Bibliothèque nationale de France)

Despite his pacifist inclinations, he ordered the continuation of the war, although the army's collapse forced him to accept the Treaty of Küçük Kaynarca in July 1774. He sought to reform the armed forces, including the Janissary corps and the navy. He also established a new artillery corps and is credited with the creation of the Imperial Naval Engineering School. He handled a series of revolts, but Russian pressure in the Crimea forced him back to war in 1787. He died in April 1789, at the age of sixty-four, in Constantinople.

Sultan Selim III

The last of the sultans during our period was the son of Sultan Mustafa III and came to the throne in April 1789. He was well-educated and a lover of the arts, although he is best remembered as a reforming sultan of the Ottoman military. However, the war against Austria and Russia dominated his early years on the throne.

At the war's conclusion, he instituted reforms to the education system and the state finances. He improved foreign relations by establishing embassies in Britain, France, Prussia, and Austria. He bypassed the Janissaries by using foreign officers to create a small corps of new troops called Nizam-I Cedid in 1797. This unit was recruited from peasant youths in Anatolia, equipped with modern weaponry, and trained in the European manner. These reforms angered the conservatives, and led by the Janissaries, they overthrew Selim in 1806. He was later murdered, and his reforms were largely dismantled.

Selim III by Konstantin Kapidagli

There were twenty-one **grand viziers** of the Ottoman Empire in this period, few lasting more than two years. They were the Sultan's prime minister, but also commanded the field army. Failure on the battlefield often led to execution or dismissal. We outline the more significant post-holders here.

Mehmed Emin Pasha (1724–1769)

Mehmed Pasha was appointed grand vizier on the outbreak of war. He was born in Constantinople into a merchant family in 1724. He spent time in India, working for the ambassador, and was appointed to the Porte on his return after writing a treatise on his travels. He served in several government posts and then in the provinces. He was appointed grand vizier after Hamza Pasha resigned due to ill health. However, he had no experience of war, and he was blamed for the army's early failures, including the supply of troops. He tried to resign, claiming ill health, and was sent to Edirne, where he was strangled. His body was buried in Edirne.

Ivazzade Halil Pasha (1724–1777)

Halil Pasha served as grand vizier from 1769. He was the son of Grand Vizier Ivaz Mehmed Pasha, known as 'Conqueror of Belgrade' after he recaptured Belgrade from the Austrians in 1739. When Grand Vizier Moldovanî Ali Pasha withdrew from the Khotyn front and the castle was lost, the path to the grand viziership was opened for him.

He was the Commander General of the Army (*Serdar-i Ekrem*) during the 1768 war. As grand vizier, he could not be blamed for the disaster at Chesma, but he was defeated at the Battle of Kagul on 1 August 1770. After being excused from military service, he was subsequently appointed to the governorships of the Sanjak of Eğriboz (eastern Central Greece), the Eyalet of Bosnia, the Eyalet of Salonika, and the Eyalet of Sivas.

Halil Hamit Pasha (1736–1785)

Halil Hamid Pasha, also known as Khaleel Hameed Basha, served as the grand vizier of the Ottoman Empire from December 1782 to April 1785. Stanford Shaw describes him as one of the outstanding reformers, inviting foreign experts, especially French ones, to the Ottoman Empire from 1784. These included artillery and engineering experts, and he was involved in establishing a new engineering school and textbooks. His support for modernisation and a conciliatory stance against Russia created enemies. He was suspected of plotting for the succession of Abdul Hamid I and the future ruler, Selim III. Halil Hamid Pasha was beheaded, and the war party rose to power, leading the Empire to war with Russia in 1787.

Koca Yusuf Pasha (1730–1800)

Koca Yusuf Pasha

Koca Yusuf Pasha was a Georgian convert to Islam who had served as the governor of the Peloponnese. He first served as grand vizier from 25 January 1786 to 28 May 1789 (during the reign of Abdul Hamid I). He became grand vizier again, serving from 12 February 1791 until mid-1792 (during the reign of Selim III). He is considered one of the best Ottoman commanders of his time despite being defeated at the Battle of Focşani.

Mandalzade Hüsameddin

Mandalzade Hüsameddin rose through the ranks from a skilled sailor to become a Mirmiran (Pasha) in 1769. In 1770, he was appointed the high admiral. The Ottoman navy, which had been neglected before his appointment, had become significantly weakened. In 1770, the Ottoman fleet, led by Hüsamaddin, clashed with the Russian fleet, led by Admiral Spiridov. Despite objections from other commanders, Hüsamaddin anchored his fleet at Chesma Bay, which led to their defeat. Following the battle, Hüsamaddin was dismissed, and in October 1770, the Algerian Hassan Pasha replaced him.

Hassan Pasha (1713–1790)

Cezayirli Gazi Hasan Pasha or Hasan Pasha of Algiers, nicknamed *Ejder-i Bahrî* (Monster of the Seas), was an Ottoman grand admiral (1770–90), grand vizier (1790), and general in the late eighteenth century. He was brought up as an enslaved Georgian in Tekirdağ and gained his naval experience with the Barbary Coast corsairs based in Algiers. He managed to extract the forces under his command from the disaster at Chesma and later dislodged the Russians from Lemnos. He was a moderate reformer who established the Naval Engineering Golden Horn Shipyard (later known as the Turkish Naval Academy) in 1773. In 1775, he successfully put down the revolt in Palestine of Zahir al-Umar, and later the Mamluk revolt in

Egypt. At the outset of the 1787 war (when he was seventy-four), he commanded Ottoman forces at the Battle of Fidonisi and the Siege of Ochakov. Famous for the domesticated lion he took everywhere, he died in 1790.

There were thirteen **Crimean Tatar khans** from 1768 to the last khan in 1783, although some served more than once. These are the most significant.

Qirim Giray (1717–1769)

Qirim Giray had been deposed as khan in 1764 but regained power in 1768. He led the first Tatar invasion of the 1768 war at the age of sixty-two. Although old for the era, De Tott described him as having 'a good shape, a noble air, easy manners, a majestic figure, a quick eye and the talent of assuming a gentle benevolence, or a commanding severity.' The raid did considerable damage and claimed a large amount of plunder, but achieved little else. He became ill during the winter weather and died at Bender.

Devlet IV Giray (1730–1780)

Devlet Giray was born in 1730, the younger son of Arslan Giray. He was appointed after the death of Qirim Giray. The Ottoman Ambassador to Russia, Ahmed Resmi Efendi, described him as 'a wretch,' one of many Girays the Sultan kept for such appointments. He was appointed khan for a second time in 1775 after successful campaigns against the Russians.

Qaplan II Giray (1739–1771)

Qaplan (Kaplan) Giray was the Crimean khan between 1769 and 1770. By this period, the khan no longer had absolute control of the khanate or the army, which was shared with two other royal leaders, the Nureddin and Kalga Sultans, and his area of control was limited to Crimea. The Tatar clans also had a degree of autonomy and did not always follow the khan. In the 1768 war, he replaced Devlet Giray as khan in 1770, led an army against the Russians in Moldavia and Transylvania, and helped defend Kili. He died in 1771.

Şahin Giray (1745–1787)

Şahin Giray

Sahin Giray was the khan from 1777 to 1782, and returned in 1782–83 to become the last khan. He studied in Greece and Venice, mastering at least four languages, before being recalled to lead the Nogai Horde. He succeeded his uncle Devlet Giray in 1777 and attempted to implement economic reforms, including restoring taxation and integrating minorities into the state system. These reforms led to rebellions by the Tatar nobility who felt their traditional privileges were being undermined. He resumed control only with Russian assistance and was eventually forced to agree to the Russian annexation. He moved to St. Petersburg but was allowed to return to Edirne in 1787. However, the Ottomans viewed him as a possible challenger to the Sultan, and he was executed in Rhodes.

François Baron de Tott (1733–1793)

De Tott was born in France into a family of Hungarian origin. He joined his father's regiment and was promoted to lieutenant in 1754. In 1755, he travelled to Constantinople as secretary to the French ambassador and was sent to Crimea to gather information about the khanate. He returned in 1767 as the French consul.

In the 1768 war, he accompanied the Crimean khan during the first significant action, providing an eyewitness account. He advised the Ottomans on strengthening the defences of the Dardanelles after 1770, building fortifications on the Bosporus, and developing a new artillery foundry. In this, he followed in the footsteps of the Count of Bonneval, who had advised on earlier artillery reforms. After the war, he continued to advise on military reform, including the artillery corps, and travelled across the empire. This included prospecting an area for the construction of a canal at Suez. He died in Hungary in 1793.

Ahmed Resmi (1694–1783)

Ahmed Resmi was born in the Cretan town of Rethymno (Resmo) in 1695 (other sources say 1700) to a family of Greek descent. On arriving in Constantinople, he rose through the ranks of the Ottoman bureaucracy, under the patronage of a circle of reformers, including two grand viziers. His literary skills attracted attention, and he became an early Ottoman diplomat, serving as ambassador to Vienna and Berlin.

During the 1768 war, he served twice as second-in-command (*Sadaret Kethüdasi*) to the grand vizier. First, with Moldovanli Ali Pasha in 1769 while the grand vizier was on the Bulgarian battlefront, and again with Muhsinzade Mehmed Pasha from 1771. His criticism of Ottoman military organisation probably kept him from achieving the top job, but his writings are important primary sources on the conflict. Ahmed Resmi acted as first plenipotentiary to the Küçük Kaynarca peace negotiations in 1774 and became one of the signatories of the resulting treaty. He continued to work behind the scenes in the Ottoman bureaucracy until he died in 1783.

Chapter Eight

The Balkans and Crimea, 1768–74

War of the Bar Confederation

The Russo-Ottoman War of 1768 has its origins in a parallel conflict known as the War of the Bar Confederation. The Confederation was an association of Polish nobles formed at the fortress of Bar in Podolia (now Ukraine) in 1768. It aimed to defend the Polish-Lithuanian Commonwealth against Russia and to oppose the Polish King Stanislaus II Augustus with Polish reformers, who were attempting to limit the power of the Commonwealth's wealthy magnates.

The once powerful Polish-Lithuanian Commonwealth was in severe decay by 1768. The king was elected by nobles who clung to their privileges, which included the power to individually veto any decision of the Polish Diet (*Sejm*). The king had no control over taxation, no effective administration, and only a small standing army. Russia in particular exploited this weakness, and during the Seven Years' War, conducted its campaigns against Prussia on Polish territory. King Stanislaus II Augustus, a former lover of Catherine II, was elected king in 1764 with Russian support, and Catherine became the de facto ruler through her minister, Nikolai Repnin. She was supported by powerful Polish families, primarily the Czartoryskis (known as 'The Family'), who held key governorships.

Austria and Prussia also had territorial ambitions in Poland, seeking to maintain the balance of power in the region and use Poland as a buffer against Russia. As Herbert Kaplan puts it, 'Geography has always been the bane of Poland. One vast plain open to invasion on all sides, she has to resist the eastward expansion of the Germans and defend herself against the westward movement of the Muscovites. In the south, Poland and the Ottoman Empire disputed for many years over the borderlands, but with the growth of Russian power, they found a common enemy.'[1]

While Catherine was not opposed to reform in Poland, she sparked the conflict by insisting on Russia's right to protect Orthodox and Lutheran religious dissidents. This also helped her internally, as she was a convert to Orthodoxy. The Confederation opposed this and, encouraged by France and Austria, declared war on Russia. They mobilised irregular troops, volunteers, and deserters from the royal army, led by Michał Jan Pac and Prince Karol Stanisław Radziwiłł. After some initial success against Russian forces, King Stanislaus Augustus sent an army under Grand Hetman Franciszek Ksawery Branicki against the main Confederation army, capturing Bar on 20 June 1768. Confederation forces and their leaders retreated into Moldavia. However, other revolts broke out, drawing in more Russian troops to suppress them.

The Confederation consisted of several smaller confederations, and there was little coordination between the armed forces; as a result, they failed to attract sufficient support from major powers. Even French financial support was sent in secret, and the French mission quickly decided that the Confederation would fail, reporting that they were in a state of disorder. Austria declined to engage, and the Papacy was distracted elsewhere.

The Russians were aware of Ottoman sensitivity, and initially ordered troops to stay fifteen miles from the border. However, that became more difficult to achieve as the Confederation forces were pushed back. Catherine sent Cossack units to suppress the insurrection, and these units encroached into Ottoman territory, sacking the village of Balta. This action strengthened the war party in Constantinople, which was fuelled by French diplomats, and persuaded the Sultan to adopt a warlike policy. The Russian ambassador to the Porte was summoned to the grand vizier and was required to answer if Russian troops would depart: 'You must say in two words, you accept the proposal, or war.' He replied that Russian troops would leave when they were finished. He and his staff were imprisoned, the traditional Ottoman method of declaring war.

The outbreak of war between the Ottomans and Russians encouraged the Confederation, and France sent Charles François Dumouriez to help reorganise their forces.[2] This strengthened their defences, but division led to further defeats, at Lanckorona on 21 May and Stałowicze on 23 October 1771. The final battle of the war was the siege of Jasna Góra, which fell on 13 August 1772. Prussia and Austria took advantage of the conflict to seize territory, which led to the First Partition of

---

1. H. Kaplan, *The First Partition of Poland*, (Columbia University Press, 1962), p. 2.

2. Dumouriez was later to achieve fame in the French Revolutionary Wars at the Battle of Valmy.

Poland, signed at Vienna on 19 February 1772. Bar Confederates taken as prisoners by the Russians, together with their families, formed the first major group of Poles and Lithuanians exiled to Siberia.

War Plans

While the Ottoman declaration of war caught the Russians unprepared, Catherine quickly assembled a new Council of State to agree on war aims. These included the recapture of the fortresses of Azov and Taganrog, which gave access to the Black Sea. Catherine referred to them as 'two jewels which I am having mounted.' The council also agreed to send a fleet into the Mediterranean (with British permission, as it would have to sail from the Baltic) and ferment revolts in Dalmatia and the Morea (Greece). The final front would be in the Caucasus, pushing into Kabardia and Georgia. Defensively, they prepared for the usual Tatar raids and an Ottoman link-up with the Bar Confederation forces. Writing to Voltaire, Catherine boasted, 'My soldiers go to war against the Turks as if they were on their way to a wedding.'[3]

Reflecting the war aims, the Russian forces were organised into three elements. The First Army (Golitsyn) of 80,000 men at Kiev (Kyiv) was tasked with capturing Khotyn and the other border forts on the Dniester River. The Second Army (Rumyantsev), comprising 40,000 men (plus Cossacks and Kalmyks), would be stationed at Elizavetgrad and Bakhmut to defend Ukraine and southern Russia. An Observation Corps (General Olits) of 10–15,000 men would defend Poland against the Bar Confederation. The First and Second Armies were ordered to support each other if the Ottomans concentrated against either army. Supply was a major concern when the armies moved onto Ottoman territory, and the First Army set off with around 40,000 men, although even that number required over 3,000 wagons.

When war was declared in 1768, the Russians faced a fundamental military problem: a lack of suitable maps. Catherine instructed her Ambassador in London, Count Chernyshov, to obtain maps of the region, as the British were taking a pro-Russian position. He commissioned Andrew Dury to create his *Map of the present Seat of War between the Russians, Poles and Turks* by June 1769. It was based on manuscripts and maps provided by Chernyshov. Dury may have given Chernyshov an early draft, as slightly earlier maps produced in Moscow draw on Dury's work. However, his map has several weaknesses, most notably the Crimea, and others later updated it in the century.

---

3. Catherine's letter to Voltaire, 15 April 1769.

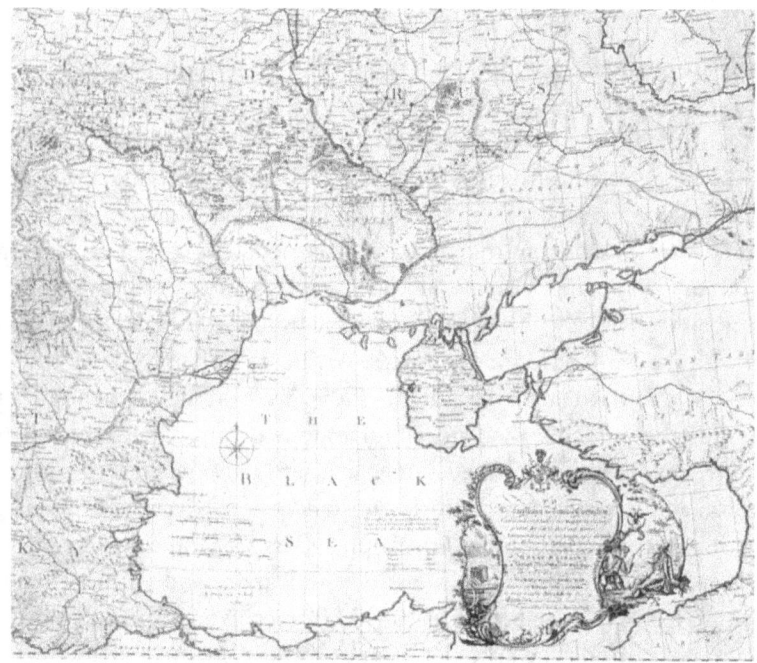

Extract from Dury's map (British Library, Map Roll 507)

Despite declaring war, the Ottomans were even less prepared than the Russians, so that the war was described by Norman Itzkowitz as a 'conflict between the one-armed and the blind.'[4] The Ottomans also envisaged three operations. The Ottoman ambassador to Russia, Ahmed Resmi, advised that approximately 40,000 troops should be dispatched to the border fortresses to deter the Russians, and that the Bar Confederation would likely provide minimal support. However, the Grand Vizier Hamza Pasha envisaged a more aggressive campaign with over 100,000 troops mobilised for an attack from Khotyn across the Dniester to capture the Russian base at Kamianets. A second army, composed mainly of some 60,000 Tatars, would raid into New Russia and Ukraine. A third army would defend Azov and make a demonstration towards Astrakhan. A total of 254,900 troops (other sources say 350,000) were to be mobilised from across the Empire, although as many as 70 per

---

4. N. Itzkowitz, *Ottoman Empire and Islamic Tradition*, (Chicago, 1972), p. 108.

cent would be raw recruits. While most would come from the Balkans and Anatolia, there were token contributions from Egypt and the Arab provinces.

Logistical challenges meant that the Ottoman army struggled to assemble quickly. Therefore, when Mehmed Emin Pasha took over as grand vizier, he reinforced the border fortresses with around 81,000 garrison troops. The field army assembled with a core of 50,000 Janissaries, although other sources indicate that the number was significantly lower, at around 15,000 when it left Constantinople, to be joined by others en route. They were supplemented by militia and volunteers to a force of well over 100,000, plus camp followers. The cavalry was estimated to be between 7,000 and 20,000, with possibly only just over 1,000 from the Kapikulu. The artillery consisted of approximately 140 guns (mostly six-pounders), 50 heavy guns, and 50 mortars, with a complement of 3,400 gunners. The Russians referenced some 200 *Zamburek* camel-mounted light guns.

Supplies were brought in from across the Empire to stock magazines and fortresses, as heavy requisitions in Moldavia and Wallachia might provoke pro-Russian sympathies. The inability to provide sufficient rations exacerbated the problem of desertion among the militia units, and Resmi references examples of commanders claiming supplies for troops that hadn't arrived.[5] Aksan references extensive lists of supplies, such as hard tack (*peksimed*), requisitioned from bakeries in Constantinople, Salonica, and Gelibolu, all far from the front line. More transport animals were needed, including 820 pairs of water buffalo and 1,450 draft horses.[6] All of this had to be paid for, and thousands of gold coins were minted. Supply problems would beset both armies, along with bad weather. Incessant rain in 1769 and 1770 caused floods that destroyed bridges and turned already poor roads into oceans of mud. This, coupled with the Russian Navy's blockade of the Dardanelles, undermined the traditional Ottoman supply strengths.

The Tatar Invasion

The Tatars were the Ottomans' traditional line of defence against the Russians since they became an Ottoman vassal in 1475. However, by this period, the Khanate was in some disarray due to internal power struggles. Resmi argued that the Tatars were the primary reason for conflict between Russia and the Ottoman Empire: 'Every time the Russians broke the articles of peace, the cause was the Tatars, who for four

---

5. A. Resmi, *A Chronicle of the 1768–1774 Russian-Ottoman War*, (Isis Press, 2011), p. 40.

6. V. Aksan, *Ottoman Wars 1700–1870*, (Pearson, 2007), p. 143.

hundred years had oppressed them, burning their house and killing their families.'[7] He claimed they had become weak and lazy, addicted to tea, coffee, and opium.

Nonetheless, Khan Qirim Giray assembled an army of between 50,000 and 100,000 Tatars (probably an exaggerated number), supplemented by 10,000 Ottoman sipahis, 20,000 Janissaries, and other auxiliaries, in what was the last great mobilisation by a Crimean khan. The plan was to take the main force in a raid into southern Poland and New Russia, while a smaller secondary force would attack the Russian Second Army at Bakhmut.

The main army left Budjak on 7 January 1769, crossed the Dniester, and concentrated at Balta (modern southwestern Ukraine) with the Ottoman forces. De Tott accompanied the khan and noted that the weather was cold and supplies limited, although he had tents carried on three camels, and swapped his Arabian horses for Circassians, able to cope with the cold and limited fodder.[8] The khan's tent could accommodate sixty people. De Tott was not impressed with the 10,000 Ottoman Sipahis who joined with the Tatar force, saying, 'It was with regret that Krim-Gueray led such bad and ill-disciplined troops to the field: he augured ill of their courage. This cavalry, accustomed to the sweets and inactivity of a long peace, not able to endure fatigue, incapable of resisting the cold, and too ill clothed likewise to support it, was effectively useless.'

They crossed into Russian territory near Orel, where the secondary force detached to attack Bakhmut. When they reached the Ingul River, the khan detached one-third of his force to raid the former New Serbia territory while the rest marched towards Fort Elizavetgrad. The weather turned even worse; thousands of mounts died, and the sixty-year-old khan became ill and had to travel by sledge. The fort had a garrison of 1,800 infantry, 2,000 light cavalry, and 2,000 Cossacks, commanded by Major-General Isakov, although their horses were equally suffering from the weather. The khan believed he wasn't strong enough to assault the fort, with De Tott saying they would have been 'cut to pieces' by a sally from the fort. The army began to withdraw with their plunder, which included over 1,000 captives, 13,000 cattle, 17,000 sheep, and 1,500 horses. The detachment attacking Bakhmut was defeated by troops from the Russian Second Army, and they retreated into Crimea with more plunder. Khan Qirim Giray reached Bender, where he died, to be replaced by Devlet IV Giray. The raid caused immense damage and gained plunder, but failed to achieve any significant objectives. Devlet did not inspire much

---

7. V. Aksan, *An Ottoman Statesman in War and Peace*, (Brill, 1995), p. 119.

8. F. De Tott, *Memoirs of Baron de Tott*, (Vol. 1, G & J Robinson, London, 1785), p. 155.

confidence in the Ottoman command, with Resmi describing him as a 'wretch' and 'initially useless.'[9]

While the main Tatar army was away, a division of Rumyantsev's Second Army, commanded by Lt. General Vernes, assembled a flotilla of 75 vessels to sail down the Don River and capture the abandoned fortress at Azov on 6 March. From there, he sent a force of Cossacks to Taganrog, which was also abandoned, and started building a harbour that would become the base for the Russian Black Sea Flotilla. The first ships were two 44-gun prams (a shallow-draught flat-bottomed ship).

Another division of the Second Army, under Lt. Gen. Berg, pushed south from Bakmut, reaching the Torets River on 1 June. Reinforced by around 60,000 Kalmyks, they advanced in two columns towards the Crimean peninsula. After driving off a Tatar reconnaissance force, they crossed into the peninsula through the Sivash Shallows, which bypassed the fortifications at Perekop. The Tatars burned the grass and fouled the water, forcing Berg to withdraw to a strong defensive position on the Kalmius River.

The Khotyn Campaign

Golitsyn's First Army of around 40,000 effectives crossed the Bug River on 25 March 1769. It included[10]:
26 line infantry regiments
3 grenadier regiments
2 cuirassier regiments
14 carabinier regiments
5 hussar regiments
100 field guns
6,000 Don Cossacks
3,000 Ukrainian Cossacks

Supply challenges delayed the crossing of the Dniester at Kalius until 15 April, reaching Khotyn on 19 April. The heavier siege guns had been left behind, and the troops carried eight days' rations, intending to take the town by storm. The Ottoman field army was struggling to cross the Danube at this date and wouldn't be able to reach Khotyn before mid-June. This left the garrison of around 20,000 men and 120 guns commanded by Hussein Pasha. A force of 10,000 cavalry commanded by Karaman Pasha had recently arrived, and there were other detachments

---

9. A. Resmi, *A Chronicle of the 1768–1774 Russian-Ottoman War*, (Isis Press, 2011), p. 46.

10. B. Davies, *The Russo-Turkish War, 1768–1774*, (Bloomsbury, 2016), p. 115.

downriver at Sorocha (13,000) and Bender (30,000). Khan Devlet IV Giray had around 80,000 Tatars near Bender.

Hussein Pasha refused a proposed sortie and ordered a large trench to be built along the south wall. The garrison mutinied and killed him, with Karaman Pasha taking over. He sortied out with his cavalry but was defeated by Prozorovskii's reserve corps near Novoselitsa. This allowed Golitsyn to move into position facing the southern walls, where the first echelon under Olits was preparing to storm the town protected by cavalry on both flanks. A three-hour bombardment caused the Ottoman troops to flee the trenches, allowing the Russians to occupy them. However, they set fire to the suburbs, halting the Russians, who, without supplies or siege guns, were forced to withdraw back across the Dniester. Golitsyn remained at Derazhna during May and June while his generals proposed various plans. He was concerned about his limited supplies and the risk of attack by Ottoman forces.

Meanwhile, in May, Rumyantsev took most of the Second Army across the Dnieper at Kriukov Shanets (Kremenchuk). His army was supposed to consist of 43,728 men, but many were inexperienced in steppe warfare, and he had an insufficient number of regular cavalry. His army included:

14 line infantry regiments
5 regular cavalry regiments
7 hussar regiments
4 pikinier regiments
40 field guns
9,000 Cossacks

Concerned that his army was stretched too thinly if the Ottoman forces combined to attack him, Rumyantsev favoured a thin defence line, with his main army acting as a mobile reserve.

Grand Vizier Emin Pasha, who was seriously ill, crossed the Danube on 2 June with the main Ottoman field army. He doubted that Golitsyn would resume the attack on Khotyn and positioned most of his forces on the Prut River at Riabaia Mogila, equidistant from Bender and Khotyn. They also had supply problems, relying on non-existent stocks at Bender. When the grand vizier asked one of his commanders, 'What do you have to say about provisions?', he received the reply, 'My lord, provisions?' followed by shrugged shoulders.[11]

---

11. A. Resmi, *A Chronicle of the 1768–1774 Russian-Ottoman War*, (Isis Press, 2011), p. 48.

Khotyn Fortress today (Rbrechko)

The Sultan favoured an offensive into Poland, although the Polish Confederates were unenthusiastic about a large Ottoman army on their territory. He sent reinforcements and supplies to Khotyn with Mehmed Pasha, including 8,000 Janissaries and 15,000 cavalry, bringing the garrison up to around 35,000 men, with a further 40,000 Tatars moving towards Khotyn.

Golitsyn detached a force to block any Ottoman raids across the Dniester and then moved his army north, crossing the river above Khotyn on 24 June. He established supply bases and advanced to the village of Pashkvitsy, six kilometres southeast of Khotyn.

On 2 July, a large Ottoman force was reported as advancing on his position. So, he formed most of his army into a square, with light cavalry on the left and a reserve on the right under Carl Stoffeln, defending a creek with a high bank. Ottoman cavalry crossed the creek and dispersed the hussars and Cossacks on the right of Stoffeln's five grenadier battalions. The grenadiers were initially overrun, but further grenadier battalions helped reform the line and push the Ottomans back. A further Ottoman attack also failed, and Golitsyn brought his square up to the bank. Golitsyn then advanced his square towards Khotyn, and was again attacked by a large force of Ottoman cavalry commanded by Mehmed Pasha. This attack was eventually dispersed with concentrated infantry and artillery fire.

Having learned that Khotyn could not be taken by storm, Golitsyn surrounded the town and began a formal siege. Field guns bombarded the town, and the roads were blocked with fieldworks to starve the garrison. Ottoman relief forces attacked these fieldworks on 22 July and managed to find a gap, which was only plugged by a counterattack from Russian heavy cavalry. Sorties from the garrison were also repulsed. A further attack on 26 July against the Russian bridges was also defeated.

Without heavy siege guns, the bombardment was having little effect, and the besiegers were running as short of supplies as the defenders. Golitsyn was also concerned about reports of a new Ottoman army advancing on his position. He therefore decided to cross back over the river on 1 August. Catherine decided to replace Golitsyn with Rumyantsev on 14 August, giving the Second Army to Petr Panin. The Sultan was equally unimpressed with his grand vizier, who was executed on 11 September and replaced by Moldovanci Ali Pasha. While Golitsyn waited for his replacement, he sent reconnaissance columns back over the river, one of which was skilfully commanded by Major-General Potemkin, who would play an increasing role in our story. He led his cavalry from the front at the Battle of Prashkovsky on 14 August and helped defeat the Moldavian Pasha on 29 August. Golitsyn wrote to Catherine, 'Our cavalry has never acted with such discipline and courage as it did under the command of the Major-General.'

Golitsyn now had two cuirassier, twelve carabinier, five hussar, three grenadier and twenty-seven line infantry regiments, plus around 9,000 Cossacks, 39,000 men in total.[12] However, the new grand vizier was also on the move with an army of around 100,000 men, throwing a bridge across the river at Khotyn and seizing the heights above Braga. From there, he was able to fire down on the Russian redoubts and repulse counterattacks by Cossacks and hussars.

Golitsyn moved his army closer to the river and prepared new field fortifications to protect his camp. He sent a strong force under Saltykov to the Babshino woods to attack the Ottoman positions in the rear. However, on 29 August, the grand vizier was on the move again, attacking the Russian camp with his main army, while Ottoman artillery bombarded it from the other side of the river. The cavalry attack failed, but Ottoman infantry in two columns made progress in the centre. The Russians were saved by Saltykov launching flank attacks on the Ottomans from the woods, forcing the Ottomans back to their bridgehead. Some 20,000 Ottoman cavalry also attempted to flank the Russians behind Babshino, but this effort was also repulsed. The Ottomans lost around 3,000 men to the Russians' 177 dead and a further 323 wounded.

The grand vizier made a further attempt across the bridge on 6 September with a force of 5,000 infantry and 7,000 cavalry, but Russian grenadiers threw this back. The Ottoman bridge collapsed during heavy rains the following night, which enabled the Russians to establish new batteries at Braga to bombard Khotyn. The Ottoman forces were short of food and fodder and demoralised by the battlefield defeat, so the grand vizier decided to abandon Khotyn and withdraw in some disorder to Hantepesi. Moldovanci Ali survived an assassination attempt but was dismissed as grand vizier by the Sultan, being replaced by Ivaz Pashazade Halil.

---

12. B. Davies, *The Russo-Turkish War, 1768–1774*, (Bloomsbury, 2016), p. 125.

Rumyantsev arrived to take command of the First Army on 18 September. He reinforced the troops pursuing the Ottomans, expanded operations into Moldavia, and linked up with the Second Army near Bender. The main elements of the army entered winter quarters at Letichev near the Bug River.

Golitsyn might be regarded as unlucky, being removed from command just as he won a victory at Khotyn. Vasiliy Kashirin summarises both sides of the balance sheet: 'The absence of a pre-developed war plan, deficiencies in the supply system of troops and the inability to use an artillery siege park significantly limited the effectiveness of Golitsyn's operations on the upper Dniester. For political and psychological reasons, this undermined Golitsyn's credibility at the imperial court and led to his removal from the post of commander-in-chief, however, it was Golitsyn's pragmatic defensive strategy that allowed him to defeat the main forces of the Ottoman army in late August – early September 1769 and force them to retreat from most of the territory of Moldova.'[13]

Moldavia and Wallachia: Larga and Kagul

After Khotyn, two columns from the First Army advanced into Moldavia to maintain pressure on the Ottomans and encourage a broader revolt against Ottoman rule. On 7 October, they captured Iași (Jassy), the capital of the Principality of Moldavia (in modern Romania). Ottoman forces withdrew to Bucharest and across the Danube into Bulgaria, while others retreated to Ibrail (Brăila), a key port on the Danube that also maintained the land link with the Crimean Tatars. This did encourage pro-Russian elements in both Moldavia and Wallachia, who provided supplies and around 6,000 volunteers for the army. Provisional governments were established under Russian generals in both principalities. Major-General Anrep occupied Bucharest on 17 (or 21) November.

Ottoman forces regrouped and sent detachments to attack Russian garrisons from their bases at Giurgiu and Ibrail on the Wallachian side of the Danube. These were largely defeated, but Anrep was not strong enough to capture either of the Ottoman bases. Both armies entered winter quarters, but that did not mean all operations ceased.

In early January 1770, Abdi Pasha advanced on the Russian base at Focșani with 4,000 cavalry and 6,800 infantry. Potemkin came to the garrison's aid with 1,500 infantry and 900 cavalry. He deployed his troops in three supporting squares,

---

13. V. Kashirin, *The Dniester Campaign of General Prince A. M. Golitsyn in 1769 and Russia's Strategy Towards the Principality of Moldavia in the Initial Period of the Russian–Turkish War of 1768–1774*, (Slavianovedenie, 2024), pp. 5-30.

instead of the usual one large square. By also abandoning the use of swine-feathers (portable stakes), he was able to move more flexibly around the battlefield. The Ottomans attacked five times, and the Janissaries managed to break into the central square. However, a counterattack by infantry drove them back, and a cavalry charge drove the Ottomans off with heavy casualties.

Reinforced with Stoffeln's division, the combined Russian force reached Ibrail on 18 January. The Russians fought their way into the town but, without siege guns, were unable to capture the fortress, which had a garrison of 15,000 troops and 80 heavy cannon. They withdrew on 21 January and moved down the Danube towards Giurgiu, burning villages. On 4 February, they attacked Giurgiu in two infantry squares supported by cavalry. They again drove the Ottomans from the trenches defending the town and repulsed a cavalry counterattack, but were unable to capture the citadel. The Moldavian Commander Abdi Pasha defended Ibrail, forcing Rumyantsev to admit that the resistance was too strong for the Russians to overcome. These rare Ottoman victories were achieved by exceptional leaders. Stoffeln abandoned the siege on 7 February and burned more villages on the Danube. While these burnings meant a loss of revenue to the Ottomans, they also destroyed Christian homes, and the empress declared the tactics barbaric. Rumyantsev agreed they were counterproductive but explained that 'in waging war against the Turks, one could not observe the rules of warfare against fellow Europeans.'[14] In March, the plague broke out in Moldavia, not helped by Stoffeln refusing to institute quarantine precautions. Ironically, he died of the plague in May. The disease spread into Ukraine and then up to Moscow, killing half the city's population, nearly 100,000 by 1773.

Heavy rain delayed the First Army's operations until 25 May, when they left Khotyn and marched south with around 25,000 men. The Second Army, under Repnin, repelled an attack from Tatar and Ottoman forces near Riabaia Mogila and was subsequently reinforced by a detachment from the First Army under General Bauer. Bauer defeated a Tatar force while crossing the Prut and then joined up with Repnin. The combined force then attacked the Ottoman camp at Riabaia Mogila, with Bauer attacking the centre while Repnin forced the Ottoman right flank. A counterattack by Ottoman cavalry was defeated, allowing the Russians to enter the Ottoman rear. They fled south, pursued by Russian cavalry.

The Ottomans regrouped on the Larga River, reinforced to a strength of around 80,000 men (primarily Tatars), awaiting the arrival of the field army. Potemkin spotted this concentration, and Rumyantsev decided he must attack before the grand vizier arrived with the field army. The Battle of Larga was fought on 7 July 1770, with the primary attack (31,000 men) on the Ottoman right flank while a

---

14. B. Davies, *The Russo-Turkish War, 1768–1774*, (Bloomsbury, 2016), p. 137.

diversionary attack with 6,000 men led by Plemiannikov attacked the trench lines in the centre. This diversionary attack commenced at 2 am, and the main attack began after dawn, in three infantry squares led by Bauer, Repnin, and Potemkin, supported by cavalry and artillery. The Ottoman cavalry counterattacked down the Babikul gully, but were repulsed by a brigade of grenadiers. The main attack managed to break into the Ottoman trenches, seize the high ground, and pour artillery fire on the Ottoman rear. After eight hours of fighting, this was too much for the Ottoman forces, who fled the field. The Tatars fled to Ismail and the Ottomans to Reni, ending joint operations between the two Ottoman forces.

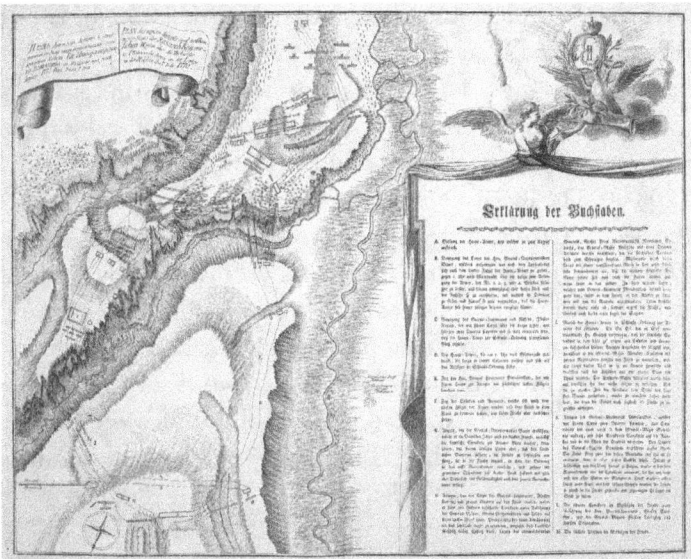

Battle of Larga («Военная энциклопедия И. Д. Сытина». (Санкт-Петербург; 1912 год)

On 12 July, the grand vizier eventually crossed the Danube and, instead of reliving the siege of Bender, he decided to attack the First Army by ordering a concentration of Ottoman forces near the Kagul River (modern Cahul and Vulcănești, in southern Moldova). Rumyantsev was camped in a vulnerable position at Grecheni, so he decided to put his train in a *wagenburg* and advance on Kagul with 25,000 men and 118 guns.

The Ottoman position faced the river using mounds known as 'Trajan's Wall,' and was covered to the south by three lines of trenches. It was a good defensive position, although with limited room to manoeuvre, the Ottoman cavalry was less effective. Kaipkaran Aga Pasha commanded the Janissaries, and Abaza Mehmed Pasha the other infantry. Abdi Pasha commanded the cavalry. The total Ottoman strength may be exaggerated in the sources, but it could have been as high as 150,000 men. The 80,000 Tatars ordered to move around the Russian rear did not reach the battlefield. The Russians would attack in five divisional squares. Bauer's division (5,000 men) were on the right flank, and Repnin's (5,000) on the left. In the centre were the divisions of Bruce (3,000), Plemiannikov (4,500), and Olits (7,500). Cavalry and guns were positioned between the squares, with the main strength focused on the Ottoman left flank.

At 5 am on 1 August 1770, the Russian squares reached Trajan's Wall and came under attack from poorly coordinated Ottoman cavalry, which was repelled with canister fire from the artillery. As Bauer's and Plemiannikov's squares reached the Ottoman trenches, 10,000 Janissaries charged from a gulley on the left flank. They broke into Plemiannikov's square, and Rumyantsev had to send in a reserve brigade to hold the line. The Janissaries fell back, pursued by Russian cavalry. While this was happening, the Ottoman right was outflanked by Bruce and Repnin, and the Ottoman forces, fearing encirclement, routed. The Ottoman dead were estimated at around 20,000. The Russians lost 353 dead and 550 wounded. Bauer's division pursued the fleeing Ottoman forces who crossed the Danube at Isaccea by boat. However, many others were stranded at Kartal because the bridge was still unfinished. Bauer attacked them, and many drowned in the river. Catherine claimed, 'Almost 2,000 Janissaries were taken prisoner on this occasion; twenty pieces of cannon, 5,000 horses, immense spoils, and a great quantity of provisions of all kinds fell into our hands.'[15] The Tatars headed to Ismail and then withdrew to Crimea. Catherine claimed that they sought Rumyantsev's permission, and many leaders were prepared to switch sides to the Russians.

---

15. Catherine to Voltaire, 9 August 1770, *Catherine the Great: Selected Letters* (Oxford), p. 95.

Battle of Kagul, July 1770 by Johann Martin Will

While the Battle of Kagul was played out, Panin's Second Army of around 45,000 men slowly marched down the Dneiper to besiege the Ottoman fortress at Bender (in modern-day Moldova), arriving on 15 July. He began a formal siege, although progress was slow due to the Ottoman bombardment and several sorties from the garrison. When Panin was told to expect reinforcements from the First Army, he decided to storm the fortress on 16 September. A massive mine was exploded under the walls, and 11,000 troops in three columns attacked the walls. A ten-hour fight in the narrow streets of the town is testament to the fierce resistance they faced. An Ottoman sortie, comprising 1,000 cavalry and 500 infantry, threatened the Russian camp, forcing troops to be diverted to defend it successfully. Because of the failure of this sortie, and with the town on fire, the remaining garrison surrendered. They had lost around 5,000 dead, and a further 11,000 went into captivity. The Russians lost 2,561 men, killed and wounded in the assault and a total of 6,236 casualties in the campaign, one-fifth of the Second Army. Panin's army retired into winter quarters on 7 November, and Panin himself retired from military service.

Bender Fortress (Author)

With the remains of the Ottoman field army in Bulgaria, the remaining fortresses on the Danube were now vulnerable to Russian attack. Repnin reached Ismail on 26 July, after defeating an attack by troops from the garrison en route. He organised an attack in four columns, but when they reached the walls, the garrison surrendered. After garrisoning the town, which would become the base of a newly formed Danube flotilla, Repnin continued to Kiliia on the Danube delta. Despite claims from Christian citizens that the Ottoman garrison had departed, Repnin found a garrison of 4,000 men who immediately sortied out when he arrived on 10 August. He settled down to a formal siege, reaching the walls on 18 August when the Ottoman commander agreed to a capitulation, with his troops marching away under parole.

The next stop was Akkerman (modern Bilhorod-Dnistrovskyi in Ukraine), located on the right bank of the Dniester Estuary, which also resisted. The detachment under Brigadier Igelstrom had no siege guns to tackle the solidly built fortress, with its stone bastions. Panin sent reinforcements from the Second Army, and the garrison surrendered on 25 September.

The final fortress was Ibrail (Brăila) on the Danube. The Russian column under Major-General Glebov bombarded the town and its garrison of 6,000 men from 27 September to 24 October. He attempted to storm the town in a night attack, but the assault columns became tangled in the darkness, and the Ottoman guns caused heavy casualties. With the threat of an Ottoman relief force, Glebov withdrew. However, the Ottoman commander, with his stores running out, decided to abandon the fortress on 9 November. This left the Russians in almost complete control of Wallachia and Moldavia, except for the eastern Danubian fortresses at Giurgiu and Tulcea. The Ottoman Sultan sent Grand Vizier Ivaz Pashazade Khalil Pasha into exile and replaced Khan Kaplan II Giray with Selim III Giray.

What became known as 'The Year of Victories' was not received as well in Vienna as it was in Moscow. With the Ottomans appearing to be on the brink of collapse and Russian troops occupying Moldavia and Wallachia, the balance of power in the Balkans was at risk. The Sultan asked Prussia and Austria to mediate through peace talks, but Austria rejected Catherine's terms as exorbitant. The Austrians strengthened their military presence in Transylvania and negotiated a treaty with their traditional enemies, the Ottomans. They did not promise joint military operations, as the Austrian army reforms were not yet complete, but it was intended to imply a threat to Russia. Prussia renewed its treaty with Russia, but suggested that it may have to retreat into neutrality if the Russians crossed the Danube. However,

Prussia and Austria were more interested in partitioning Poland, and the Austrians simply promised to encourage the Sultan to enter into direct peace talks, mediated by Austria.

The Danube Front, 1771

The new grand vizier, Silahdar Mehmed Pasha, the former Pasha of Bosnia, adopted a different strategy from his predecessors. He reinforced the garrisons on the northern bank of the Danube at Turnu and Giurgiu, as well as the major fortresses on the southern bank, with regular troops wherever possible. The field army, numbering around 45,000, was held in reserve at Babadagh (Northern Dobruja). The new khan brought 7,000 Tatars to the field army, and Moldavanci Ali Pasha had 40,000 men to defend the Dardanelles against the Russian fleet. The strategy was to launch small raids across the Danube and use the northern bank fortresses for larger incursions into Wallachia.

The Russian First Army was positioned on the strategic defensive along the Danube to counter these raids and launch its own incursions in response. This required Rumyantsev to spread his smaller army thinly along the 600-kilometre line, resulting in supply challenges. These were exacerbated by the plague in Moldavia and Wallachia, and a private contractor, Baron Hartenberg, was used to obtain rations and move them using nearly 4,000 wagons. These factors meant the conflict on this front was mainly a war of outposts. The Ottomans were experienced in crossing the Danube, and the Russians countered this by creating their own Danube flotilla, which eventually numbered some 67 ships of various sizes, with a total of 174 cannons.

To strengthen his position, Rumyantsev sent Olits to capture Giurgiu on 17 February. Without siege guns, he was forced to storm the town using four columns, heavily outnumbered by the defenders. They managed to seize the outer trenches, but the citadel held out until its powder vault exploded and the garrison was forced to surrender. Olits, who was unwell at the start of the campaign, returned to Bucharest, where he died. The new Wallachian Corps commander, Major-General Gudovich, advanced on the remaining fortress at Turnu, but decided it could not be taken without a lengthy siege. Olits had left a garrison of fewer than 400 men at Giurgiu, and on 25 May, the Ottomans brought forces from Rusçuk on the southern bank over the river. They opened fire on the outer walls and threw back a sortie from the garrison, pushing them back into the town. The garrison surrendered on 29 May, just days before Repnin's relief column arrived.

The Ottomans deployed approximately 14,000 men in Giurgiu and used it as a base to launch attacks into Wallachia, supported by raids along the river. A 10,000-strong force under Ahmed Pasha threatened Bucharest, but was stopped by

Repnin and Potemkin at the Sambor River on 10 June. These actions convinced Rumyantsev that he must retake Giurgiu. After Repnin became ill, the command was given to Lieutenant General Essen, who marched on the town with 6,000 men. He stormed Giurgiu on 7 August, but none of his three assault columns could break in, and with all three commanders wounded and one-third of his command casualties, he retreated.

In October, Ahmed Pasha led a force of 8,000 infantry and up to 40,000 cavalry towards Bucharest. Essen had 13,000 troops to stop them at Vacaresti Monastery, four kilometres from Bucharest. A light battalion got around the rear of the Ottoman infantry while Essen's main square hit the Ottoman infantry, throwing them into confusion. Ahmed Pasha sent his cavalry around the Russians to cross the Dimbovița River and cut the road to Bucharest. However, the Russian reserve broke up the Ottoman cavalry, which fled south with the infantry. The pursuit reached Giurgiu and found most of the garrison had fled. The fortress was back in Russian hands.

West of Bucharest, Potemkin had been raiding across the Danube with a modest force. He burned Ottoman magazines, captured ships, and brought Christian inhabitants back over the river. Retaliatory raids by the Ottomans were also defeated. In the east, there were similar raids by Bauer's troops against Hârșova. A larger raid by Major-General Weissman destroyed several Ottoman strong points and captured the field army's headquarters at Babadagh. This ended any hope of launching a major Ottoman assault over the Danube in 1771, plus the grand vizier was distracted by a Mamluk revolt in Egypt.

Rumyantsev has been criticised for not exploiting his victories with a major assault across the Danube. However, he was short of ships to move large numbers of troops in one move, and he had successfully carried out the War Council's strategy for the year.[16] The terrain in Bulgaria was also very different to the plains of Wallachia. Rumyantsev reported, 'Steep mountains and deep pits define its conditions. We had taken entire camps, baggage trains, and artillery from the enemy, but there was no possibility to defeat entirely his troops, who found shelter in forests and ravines where our cavalry and infantry could not move.'[17] Fever was also endemic in the principalities during the summer months, which disabled many troops, including Potemkin, who almost died. He didn't rely on treatment from army doctors; instead, he put himself into the care of two Cossacks, reflecting his

---

16. B. Davies, *The Russo-Turkish War, 1768–1774*, (Bloomsbury, 2016), pp. 171-172.

17. V. Aksan, *Ottoman Wars 1700–1870*, (Pearson, 2007), p. 156.

association with them. They called him 'Gritsko Nechosa' (Grey Wig) when he became an honorary Zaporogian Cossack in April 1772.[18]

Crimea

The Russian victories in Moldavia had already brought some of the *mirzas* (nobles) into negotiations, with the aim of breaking from the Ottoman Empire. While the Nogais were prepared to ally with Russia, the Crimean Tatars would be unlikely to make the break without an invasion. The Second Army, now commanded by Dolgorukov, was therefore tasked with invading Crimea. He had around 53,000 men and had learned from the previous campaigns in 1737 and 1738, which had failed because of supply challenges.

Dolgorukov's plan involved his main force breaking through the Perekop Line that fortified the entrance to Crimea. A subsidiary attack under Major-General Scherbatov would cross the Sivash marshes, supported by the Azov Flotilla (Rear Admiral Alexei Senyavin). Lieutenant General Osterman had 21,000 men to defend the Ukrainian Line, and Major-General Wasserman would cordon off any attack from the garrison at Ochakov (Ochakiv) on the Sea of Azov to the east. The khan and much of the Tatar army were with the Ottoman field army at Babadagh, leaving reduced garrisons under Ibraim Pasha in Crimea. It was estimated that some 55,000 men held the Perekop Line, including 7,000 Ottoman troops. The seven-kilometre wall was 8.5 meters high, faced with a ditch, but there were only five batteries and parts of the wall had fallen into disrepair.

Dolgorukov reached the Perekop Line on 12 June. He sent a diversionary attack on the eastern end of the wall while his main force attacked the western end in three columns. Both attacks breached the wall, and the Ottomans fell back to the main fort at Or-Kapi, which surrendered on 15 June. Scherbatov's troops landed on Arabat Spit on 13 June, and captured the Arabat Fortress on 17 June. The Azov Flotilla supported the assault and fought off a weak Turkish naval force. Most of the Ottoman fleet was concentrated in the Aegean at this time. Encountering little resistance, Scherbatov moved down the coast and captured Kerch and the Ottoman fortress at Yenikale on the other side of the Kerch Straits. This enabled Russian ships to enter the Black Sea, a significant Russian objective.

Khan Selim III Giray had returned to Crimea when he heard of the invasion, but did not take the field. A Russian cavalry detachment attempted to capture him in his capital at Bakhchysarai, but he fled to Constantinople. Dolgorukov took his main force to Kaffa, the main Ottoman port. He bombarded the port

---

18. S. Montefiore, *Prince of Princes: The Life of Potemkin*, (Phoenix Press, 2000), p. 86.

and fortress, forcing the Ottoman fleet to disperse. The trenches defending the town were quickly captured, and Ibraim Pasha surrendered the fortress on 30 June. Dolgorukov's rapid campaign had cut off Crimea from Constantinople, and the remaining Crimean mirzas came to his camp to request that the empress take Crimea under her protection. Khan Selim abdicated, and Sahip Giray was elected as the new khan.

The Fortress at Kaffa by Mikhail Ivanov (1783)

1772 and peace talks

With the First Partition of Poland agreed between Prussia, Austria and Russia, the Austrians abandoned their unlikely pact with the Ottomans. In March 1772, the grand vizier started peace talks with Rumyantsev at Giurgiu. An initial armistice was agreed on 30 May with support from Prussian and Austrian envoys. The substantive negotiations for a peace treaty started in August at Focşani. Grigory Orlov led the Russian negotiators, accompanied by Aleksei Obreskov, who had been released from his prison cell in Constantinople. Catherine's instructions were to reduce the Ottoman ability to attack Russia and to provide compensation for the costs of the war. This compensation included territory on the Steppe up to Azov and in the Caucasus. However, the sticking point was the independence of the Crimean Khanate and the Nogai hordes.

Events in Poland and Sweden distracted the Russians, and Orlov used the opportunity to deliver an ultimatum and abandon the talks. However, Panin and Obreskov wanted to continue talking. When the grand vizier approached Rumyantsev in September about a further armistice, agreement was quickly reached on a new round of talks in Bucharest. The Ottomans were in no position to resume the war, and Rumyantsev's army was also weakened by combat and the plague. They agreed to an armistice until 21 March 1773. This time, the Ottomans recognised that the new Crimean khan was likely to sign a peace treaty with the Russians irrespective of the Ottoman position. However, it was Obreskov's demands for free navigation rights on the Black Sea and control of Kilburn, Kerch, and Yenikale, providing unfettered access to the Black Sea, which proved the sticking point. The talks collapsed in January 1773. Ahmed Resmi commented in his chronicles that 'it was as plain as day to everyone that, in a word, there would be no better peace settlement than this were we to fight ten years hereafter.'[19]

A year without serious fighting provided a valuable breathing space for Rumyantsev, who needed to restock his supplies and bring in recruits. The costs of the war were mounting on the Russian treasury, and some troops had to be diverted in case war broke out against Sweden. There were Cossack disturbances, the plague, inflation, and declining tax revenues to add to the Russian state's challenges.

Emelian (Yemelyan) Pugachev

For the remainder of the war, the Russians would be distracted by the Pugachev Rebellion. This event originated on the Orenburg Line, Russia's eastern border, and therefore falls outside the scope of this study. However, a brief overview of one of the most serious rebellions in Russian Imperial history is necessary to understand its impact on the Russo-Ottoman War. In September 1773, a disaffected Russian Cossack officer, Emelian (Yemelyan) Pugachev, proclaimed himself Peter III. He claimed he had survived an assassination attempt (even though the real Peter III had been dead for a decade). He gathered support from discontented peasants, Cossacks, and non-Russian minorities, including Bashkirs, Tatars and Kalmyks. The rebels captured Samara and burnt Kazan.

Danube Front 1773

When the peace talks failed, Catherine pressed Rumyantsev to cross the Danube and attack the Ottoman field army, which was concentrated at Shumla. He, supported by his divisional commanders, Weissman, Saltykov, and Potemkin, believed they had insufficient forces to undertake such a bold operation without weakening their defences in Wallachia. He proposed limited strikes across the river as he had done in 1771, while he built up his strength. However, the empress rejected this plan, and Ottoman raids into Wallachia reinforced the case for destroying the Ottoman army.

---

19. A. Resmi, *A Chronicle of the 1768–1774 Russian-Ottoman War*, (Isis Press, 2011), p. 65.

Potemkin seized Hârşova at the end of April, and the newly arrived Lieutenant General Suvorov took a small force on an amphibious diversionary attack on Turtucaia (Tutrakan, Bulgaria). The preparations were spotted by an Ottoman reconnaissance force that nearly overran Suvorov's camp, potentially cutting short what was to become an illustrious career. However, Suvorov's crossing still succeeded on 21 May, and he captured Turtucaia by attacking it in three squares with the Astrakhan regiment, three squadrons of cavalry, and a regiment of Cossacks. They cleared the Ottoman camps and burnt the town. The Ottomans lost around 1,500 killed and 80 ships, along with 16 guns. The Russian dead totalled 26 men. Suvorov's first action against the Ottomans was a model amphibious landing against an enemy five times larger, and his training had enabled the troops to flexibly shift between columns and squares as the tactical situation demanded.

The action at Turtucaia had limited strategic value, as the crossing point at Hârşova was deemed unsuitable for the First Army. Instead, Rumyantsev decided to cross at Gurobaly, where the Danube was only one kilometre wide, with islands to hide the boats. The Ottomans had approximately 6,000 troops at Gurobaly, with an additional 50,000 in two camps near Silistra, 30 kilometres away. Rumyantsev concentrated 21,000 men and 74 guns for the crossing, supported by a diversionary attack on both sides. On 16 June, Weissman attacked the eastern flank of the Ottoman camp at Gurobaly while Potemkin landed in front of the camp. There was limited resistance, and the Ottoman garrison fled, allowing Rumyantsev to bring his remaining regiments across the river by 22 June. Potemkin and Weissman advanced on Silistra, fighting off flanking attacks. However, when they seized the high ground above the town, they realised that they had insufficient strength to capture the fortress, which had a garrison of 30,000. With two Ottoman forces comprising upwards of 70,000 men coming from Shumla, it was decided to retreat to the Danube for a return crossing. Weissman was tasked with covering the withdrawal, and his division defeated an Ottoman attack at Küçük Kaynarca on 3 July. This allowed the Russian army to cross the river, although Weissman was killed in the action. Meanwhile, Suvorov launched another attack on Turtukai on 28 June, this time achieving surprise and driving the Ottoman force away, before defeating a counterattack. He was decorated for this action and took command at Hârşova.

The breakout had failed, although the Ottoman forces had been depleted in the actions fought. The problem for the Russians was that the new Ottoman commanders were less likely to risk a major battle, and local garrison commanders, often provincial *ayans*, were defending their territory with their own troops and showed greater persistence.[20] The empress reluctantly agreed to a further levy of

---

20. *Ayans* were local notables or warlords who held varying degrees of authority in provincial towns and districts.

conscripts for the army, telling Rumyantsev that she expected a sound campaign plan for the following year.

For the rest of 1773, the campaign again returned to a war of outposts, with Rumyantsev reinforcing his garrisons on the Danube and sending raids across it. The Ottomans were encouraged by the Russian withdrawal at Silistra, and the grand vizier attacked Hârșova, which Suvorov held with only 4,000 men. Ahmed Pasha's advanced guard (7–10,000 men) was lured into a trap using concealed redoubts by Suvorov, and were routed. This encouraged Rumyantsev to join Suvorov's forces, which included units commanded by Ungern and Dolgorukov, and they captured Karasu on 17 October. Rumyantsev was now seriously ill, and his plans were left to divisional commanders. Saltykov established batteries on an island opposite Rusçuk and sent raiding parties across the Danube. Potemkin launched a similar operation against Silistra, but coordination was poor, and these operations failed to deliver a wider opportunity against the Ottoman field army. Heavy rains also hampered operations, and the troops were short of supplies, resulting in illness. Most forces, therefore, withdrew into winter quarters.

Spring 1774 campaign

Catherine pressed Rumyantsev for a major offensive into Bulgaria in 1774 that would bring the Sultan to the peace table. It was eventually agreed to blockade the Ottoman fortresses at Rusçuk and Silistra, with the aim of destroying the Ottoman field army at Shumla. Sultan Mustafa III died on 21 January 1774 at the Topkapi Palace, and was succeeded by his less warlike brother Abdul Hamid I. This gave the peace party in Constantinople, led by the grand vizier, an opportunity to press for a return to peace negotiations.

The Russian First Army had around 55,000 men available for the offensive. In April, Kamenskii took over 10,000 troops across the Danube at Isaccea and advanced towards Bazarjik. The plan was to rendezvous with Suvorov, who crossed at Hârșova with 15,000 men, reaching Cherovody on 27 May. The rest of the First Army blockaded Rusçuk (Saltykov's division) and Silistra (Glebov's division). They joined up on 19 June and advanced towards Kozludzha (modern Suvorovo). On 20 June, 12 kilometres from Kozludzha, in the Deliorman Forest, they were attacked by the Ottoman field army of 15,000 cavalry and 25,000 infantry, commanded by Reis Efendi Abdurrezak. The Russians were initially pushed out of the forest, but they recovered and formed squares. Three attacks were made on Suvorov's vanguard, which were beaten off, possibly with support from Kamenskii, who claimed the victory. The Ottoman forces were routed, and the road to Shumla lay open. However, Kamenskii rested his exhausted troops for four days, and Suvorov was forced to hand over his command to Miloradovich due to illness.

The Battle of Kozludzha 1774 (I.F. Anting)

Kamenskii reached Shumla on 28 June and began a siege. The garrison made three sorties, and a relief force was defeated south of Shumla at Chaplyk-Kovak. With supplies running low, the garrison started to desert. The Ottomans were unable to mobilise an army large enough to challenge even the depleted Russian forces. Desertion was endemic, and supplies were regularly looted. The grand vizier accepted the Russian terms for an armistice and peace talks. On 16 July, the Ottoman representatives arrived at Rumyantsev's headquarters in Küçük Kaynarca to begin negotiations.

Chapter Nine

War in the Caucasus

The Caucasus is a region spanning Eastern Europe and Western Asia, situated in the 'lands in-between' the Black Sea and the Caspian Sea, and between Europe and Asia, and a crossing place of cultures.[1] It is divided into the North Caucasus and the South Caucasus, separated by the Greater Caucasus mountain range to the north and the Lesser Caucasus mountain range to the south.

Russia had been expanding towards the Caucasus from the sixteenth century. Cossacks established settlements on the Don River as early as 1550, and Astrakhan was conquered in 1556. This gave Russia a base at the northern end of the Caspian Sea. Peter the Great advanced down the coast of the Caspian Sea during the Russo-Persian War (1722–23), but returned the territory in 1735. The Ottomans viewed the Caucasus as part of the Crimean Khanate and generally worked through the khan. There was a tradition that all the khans, before they were promoted, were sent to a local Circassian tribe to receive their education. This tradition (called Atalık or P'vr) helped to form a strong connection between the Khanate and the Western Caucasus.

---

1. T. De Waal, *The Caucasus* (Oxford, 2010), p. 1.

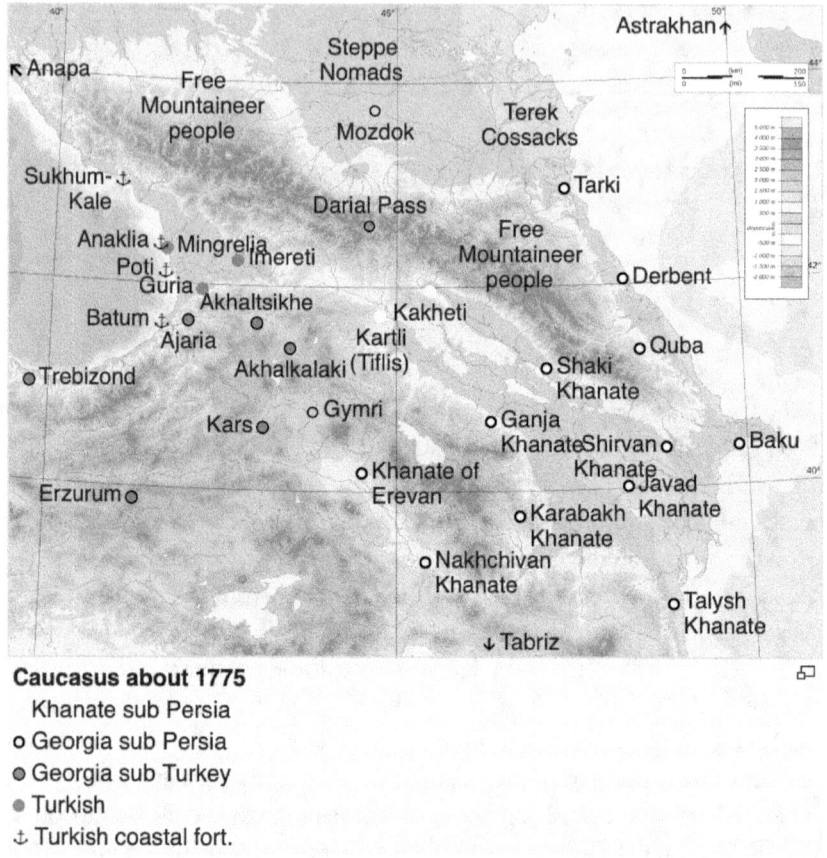

Map of the Caucasus 1775 (Bourrichon)

At the outbreak of war in 1768, the Russians primarily saw a campaign in the North Caucasus as a way of diverting Ottoman military resources. Kabardia was a weak buffer state between the Russian and Ottoman empires, split between different factions, with Cossack units serving in the pro-Russian faction. This had enabled the Russians to edge closer to Kabardian territory, with settlements on the Kuban River. Kizlar, on the Terek River estuary, was founded in 1736. The Russian fortress of Mozdok was built on the other side of the Terek River in 1763. It was attacked by Kabardian nobles who were angry at the incursion into their traditional pasturelands, and because Mozdok had become a refuge for their runaway enslaved people. Catherine resettled part of the Volga Cossacks to the area, establishing the Mozdok Regiment.

Major-General I. F. Medem was transferred to Mozdok in April 1769 to command a force of 1,600 Cossacks as well as one regiment from the Astrakhan garrison, two squadrons of dragoons, and two squadrons of Georgian hussars.² Medem supplemented this 3,000-strong force by raising local volunteers and recruiting 20,000 Kalmyk auxiliaries under Khan Ubashi. He was tasked with defending Mozdok and raising the tribes of the Caucasus against the Ottomans.

On 29 April, Khan Ubashi (who had a small force of Russians attached) defeated around 6,000 Kuban Tatars near the Kalaus River. They advanced into the Beshtava Mountains, receiving support from the pro-Russian Kabardian factions and attacking the pro-Ottoman factions, who quickly submitted. On 21 June, they reached the Kuban River, and had to defeat another force of Kuban Tatars before they were able to force a crossing. Medem returned to Mozdok to deal with a Chechen uprising, and Ubashi tried to capture the Kuban Tatar capital at Kopyl, but it was too heavily fortified. In early 1770, Ubashi fell out with Medem over the granting of grazing lands to German colonists, and took his horde east across the Volga to their traditional homelands in Dzungaria.

With the Terek Line secured, the Russians saw a strategic opportunity to link up with the Christian kingdom of Georgia. The Transcaucasian Corps, commanded by Count Todtleben, with nearly 4,000 men, crossed the Caucasus Mountains through the Darial Pass in the summer of 1769.³

Count Gottlieb Totleben

He joined with King Heraclius (Irakli) II of the Kingdom of Kakheti and Kartli-Kakheti, who hoped to reconquer the Ottoman-held southern Georgian lands. He was soon joined by King Solomon I of Imereti, who had been fighting the Ottomans for ten years. However, the kings wanted to create an independent Georgia, while Todtleben wanted them to swear allegiance to Russia. This led Todtleben to engage in the internal politics of Georgia, a move opposed by other Russian officers. A joint force did capture the Ottoman fortresses at Sadgueri and Atsquri. King Heraclius defeated a twenty-thousand-strong Ottoman army at the Battle of Aspindza on 20 April 1770, after being abandoned by the Russian troops. The Georgians managed to destroy the bridge over the

---

2. B. Davies, *The Russo-Turkish War, 1768–1774*, (Bloomsbury, 2016), p. 132.

3. Count Gottlieb Todtleben was a Saxon officer who entered the Russian service during the Seven Years' War. He distinguished himself at the Battle of Kunersdorf and was promoted to General. However, after briefly capturing Berlin he retreated and was convicted of treachery. Pardoned by Catherine, he was recalled in 1768.

River Kura at the town, separating the Ottoman force and then executing a surprise attack.

This victory ended any hopes for Todtleben's plotting, so he crossed into Imereti and helped King Solomon capture the Ottoman fortresses at Shorapani and Baghdati before recovering the capital, Kutaisi, on 6 August 1770. He defeated 25,000 Ottoman troops as he marched on the Black Sea port of Poti, but the subsequent siege went badly, and he fell out with King Solomon. Totleben was recalled from Georgia in January 1771 and assigned to lead a division at Warsaw, where he soon died. His replacement, General Alexey Sukhotin, lost half the army to disease, and the War Council began to lose interest in the campaign, withdrawing to the Mozdok Line in 1772. Heraclius and Soloman continued to fight the Ottomans, but were abandoned by the Russians in the subsequent peace negotiations that ended the war.

It is argued that a more competent commander than Todtleben could have achieved considerable success, even with the limited forces at his disposal. Lang, based on a French eyewitness account, says, 'Supported by the united strength of Georgia and Imeret'i, he could certainly have stormed the citadel of Akhaltsikhe and advanced on Erzerum, as Paskevich was to do in 1828. In the event, Todtleben's deplorable conduct of affairs imperilled the safety of his troops, rendered decisive victory impossible, strained Russo-Georgian relations, aggravated the discord between the autonomous princes of Transcaucasia.'[4]

The Georgians felt betrayed by the treaty, complaining, 'Now you are leaving Georgia, to the extreme despair of our subjects.' In late 1777, the Russian Caucasian army was divided into two. Suvorov commanded the Kuban army while General Yakobi became the commander of the Caucasus army. A new line of fortified positions was constructed and settled with Cossacks from the Volga region and other areas. Yakobi fortified the Mozdok-Rostov line, while Suvorov completed the fortified line from Kerç to Kuban River by January 1778. He then extended the fortifications between Mozdok and the Caspian Sea.

In 1782, Russia attacked Baku with twelve ships, but was unable to break the resistance and had to retreat. Also in 1782, Catherine accepted a proposal to bring Georgia under her protection, and the Treaty of Georgievsk was signed on 24 July 1783. In October 1783, two battalions and four batteries were sent to Tiflis under the command of General Samoilov. The Ottomans stirred up rebellions until an agreement was reached that they would cease hostilities. In return, Russian forces

---

4. D. Lang, *Count Todtleben's Expedition to Georgia 1769–1771 according to a French Eyewitness*, (Bulletin of the School of Oriental and African Studies, University of London, Vol. 13, No. 4, 1951), pp. 878–907.

in Georgia would not exceed 3,000 men, and the Georgians would not threaten Ottoman territories.

In 1785, the first signs of a united Islamic resistance to Russian expansionism in the Northern Caucasus appeared under the leadership of Imam Mansur. His real name was probably Ushurma, a Chechen born in Aldy (modern Grozny) in 1760. His origins are unclear, and there are other claims about his background, including the somewhat fantastic idea that he was an Italian.[5] He claimed to have a vision of the Prophet, saying, 'O believers! Know that your life is full of ignorance, and that you have committed sins by drinking alcohol and smoking tobacco. Now you have an opportunity to rectify your mistakes and to find a way out. Give alms to the poor, and fight against the enemy. Anything Russian is forbidden, as is any manner resembling that of the Russians.' The Ottomans were not enthusiastic about this revolt, as they worried it might spark a new conflict with Russia. There were also worries that Mansur might shift the allegiance of the Caucasian tribes from the Ottoman Empire to himself.

Potemkin sent a force of 3,000 troops under Colonel Nikolai de Pieri to capture Mansur in June 1785. They burned the village of Aldy, but when withdrawing, they were ambushed in the nearby forest, losing 745 men (including Pieri) and a further 162 captured. This success brought recruits to Mansur, who besieged Kislar on 5 July 1785, but found the fortress too strong. He did gain a foothold on the Vladikavkaz-Mozdok line later that month by capturing Kumkalesi, but couldn't exploit the victory in a second failed attempt to capture Kislar. Potemkin sent a much larger force to the region, winning a series of victories that culminated in the Battle of Tatartup in November 1785. These defeats led to Mansur losing the support of the nobles, but he continued with a low-level conflict, inflicting defeats on Russian garrisons. This largely died out in 1786, when Mansur sought refuge in Ottoman territory.

When war broke out between the Ottomans and Russians again in 1787, the Caucasus was not a major theatre. However, the Ottomans established an alliance with Mansur. In 1787, the Russians sent an expedition to capture the Ottoman fortress of Anapa, consisting of 8,000 men and 35 guns. Situated on the Taman Peninsula, twenty miles from the mouth of the Kuban River, Anapa was a maritime stronghold and served as the basis of Turkish influence and power in the northern Caucasus. The loss of Crimea cut off the Ottomans' land route, increasing the importance of Anapa, and French engineers improved the fortifications. Chechen forces harassed the expedition, and the rearguard was almost wiped out in a night attack. The Russians withdrew back over the Kuban River.

---

5. A. Özer, *The Ottoman-Russian Relations Between the Years 1774-1787*, (Bilkent University, 2008), p. 96.

A further attempt was made the following year, commanded by General Tekeli. It reached the fortress, but was ambushed by Chechen forces on the flanks as the Janissaries sortied out of the fortress. Tekeli withdrew across the Kuban River. A final attempt was made in 1790 with a force of 12,000 men led by General Bibikov. The garrison had been reinforced to a strength of 15,000 men commanded by Battal Hussein Pasha. Bibikov fought off Ottoman and Chechen attacks on his column, arriving at Anapa on 24 March. He stormed the fortress, but the attack was driven off, and again the Chechens attacked his flanks. Having lost 5,000 casualties, he withdrew.

The Ottomans sought to exploit their victory, and landed an expeditionary force on the coast under the command of Batal Pasha. He managed to concentrate his attack on the Russian position on the banks of the Podpaklea River. This was held by General Hermann, a Saxon in Russian service, with 3,600 men and six guns. The Ottoman attack was beaten off, and the retreating troops were caught by another Russian force and destroyed. The Russians then amassed a much stronger army in January 1791 commanded by Count Goudovitch, with 15 infantry battalions, 3,000 Jagers, and 54 cavalry squadrons. They stormed Anapa in June, capturing the town at a cost of more than 4,000 casualties. They also captured Sheikh Mansur, who was in the fortress. He was 'inspected' by Catherine in St. Petersburg and imprisoned. He died in April 1794.

The Russians strengthened their fortifications and forcibly resettled Don Cossacks into the region. The subsequent peace treaty made no significant changes to the respective positions in the Caucasus.

Chapter Ten

Naval Warfare and the Mediterranean

As a largely landlocked nation, Russia was late in developing a navy. Peter the Great established the modern Russian Navy in 1696, with a small force built for the war against the Ottomans around the fortress of Azov. Galley squadrons were established to challenge Sweden during the Great Northern War (1700–1721). Still, it was the construction of St. Petersburg and the nearby naval base at Kronstadt that enabled the development of a balanced fleet. By the 1750s, the Russian Navy had 130 sailing vessels, including 36 ships of the line and nine frigates. Russian ships tended to be heavier, with larger guns and smaller crews than those of their Ottoman counterparts. The Russians had no maritime tradition, which made shipbuilding a challenging endeavour, and they struggled to find the right timber and prepare it properly. This meant the lifespan of a Russian ship was significantly shorter than that of other European nations, which had developed copper protection for their hulls.[1] The Russian Navy also relied heavily on 250 galleys, which were useful for coastal warfare, particularly in rivers and estuaries where deep-draught ships could not operate. Officers were recruited from the nobility, although foreign officers were also recruited for their experience. Russian ships could be short on officers, and conscripted sailors often had no maritime experience.

The Ottoman Navy had a long history, dating back to when it first crossed the Straits into Europe. They developed bases on the northern Black Sea coast from the late fifteenth century and subsequently captured bases across the Balkan coastline and into the Levant. North African vassals added to the fleet and provided some of its most famous admirals. Ottoman ships operated in the Persian Gulf, India,

---

1. K. Muller, *Der Vorstoß der russischen Flotte in den Griechischen Archipel, 1769 bis 1775* (Redaktionsbüro OSTPROJEKT, 2013), p. 24.

and as far as Indonesia. By 1768, the Ottoman Navy had two fleets, the Great Fleet (*Kebir Donanma*) consisting of sailing warships, and the Slim Fleet (*Ince Donanma*) consisting of galleys and gunboats. In 1768, there were only five 74-gun ships of the line, and one of those was in poor condition. These were supported by nine smaller ships of the line (54 and 60 guns), which were more suited for peacetime operations. There were also three *karavels*, with 48 guns, often confused as frigates. In Western sources, Ottoman ships are described as having high sterns and decks and being cumbersome to sail. However, modern research questions this assessment, instead pointing to weaknesses in the single-framed hulls, 'almost like eggshell', and that ships carried fewer guns than their capacity.[2] Ottoman guns were usually cast in bronze, a higher-quality material that, although more expensive, may explain the under-armament of ships. The Ottoman Navy was designed for coastal operations and supporting the army in amphibious operations.

Naval expedition to the Mediterranean

The Russian war plan in 1768 included encouraging revolts against Ottoman rule in Dalmatia and Morea (modern Greece), which had their genesis in earlier links with Orthodox Christian groups in the Balkans during Peter the Great's rule. This would later become known as Catherine's 'Greek Project,' under which she claimed it was Russia's duty to 'liberate' Orthodox people under Ottoman control. She was encouraged to develop this policy by her close confidant, Voltaire, who urged Catherine through an ode to 'revenge Greece [and] drive out the unworthy.' At this stage, the policy aimed to show the flag, hoping that the sight of Russia, the Greeks' Orthodox saviour, would rally the Greeks to their liberator's side and disrupt the Ottoman war effort in the West. It was also aimed at drawing Ottoman warships from the Black Sea.

Russian agents had been sent to the Mani area of the Peloponnese in the mid-1760s to ally with the strongest local military leaders, and notable Greeks had approached various Russian contacts to discuss plans for the liberation of Greece. There had also been an insurrection in Cyprus in 1765, which developed due to similar grievances.[3] This emphasises that Russia was taking advantage of existing economic grievances and internal power struggles in the Morea, not simply an outburst of religious nationalism. However, not all Christians participated in

---

2. E. Yener, *Ottoman Seapower and Naval Technology during Catherine II's Turkish Wars 1768–92*, (International Naval Journal, Vol. 9, Issue 1, 2016).

3. B. Gundogdu, *Ottoman Constructions of the Morea Rebellion*, 1770s (University of Toronto, 2012), pp. 123–128.

this rebellion, which significantly aided the Ottomans in suppressing the uprising quickly. It is often assumed that there were two distinct societies separate from one another. However, the available sources do not recognise the existence of any united/homogenous group of people which can be delineated according to their religion. There are recorded instances of Greeks of modest means providing intelligence to the Ottoman troops. Religion was not a sufficient cause to unite all Greeks.

Further agents were dispatched to Bosnia, Herzegovina, Montenegro, Albania, Crete, and the Morea upon the outbreak of war. To support these efforts, sending a fleet into the Mediterranean posed a challenge for the Russian Navy, which lacked access to ports on the Black Sea. Even if it had access, the Ottomans could block access through the Straits. In the absence of such access, Count Aleksei Orlov was appointed to lead an expedition into the Mediterranean using elements of the Baltic Fleet in January 1769. He and his brothers, Grigory and Fedor, had been working on this project since 1762, building contacts across the region. Orlov had no naval experience, but his knowledge of the area and intelligence network made him politically essential to the expedition. His instructions were to create an effective diversion, and Catherine's 'Manifesto to the Greeks and the southern Slavs' stated that the Russian fleet was an opportunity to struggle for their freedom. The activities of the Orlov brothers had not gone unnoticed by the Ottomans. They adopted a carrot-and-stick approach, arresting suspected conspirators and instructing their governors to avoid provocations. Venice was also concerned about how a Russian fleet would impact its interests in the region. Still, the British ambassador to St. Petersburg didn't believe it would affect any of their treaties with the Ottomans.[4] However, he later wondered if a Greek revolt might spread to Venetian territories.

For the Baltic Fleet, a Mediterranean expedition involved a journey from Kronstadt, across the North Sea, through the Channel, and past Gibraltar. This all required at least the passive cooperation of the Royal Navy, which was forthcoming during this period. The British had signed a trade agreement in 1765, and although that had not developed into a full alliance, it was enough for the British to rebuff French efforts to get them to block the Russian expedition, and provide support for repairs and stores. The First Squadron, commanded by Admiral G. A. Spiridov, included seven ships of the line, supported by transports, galleys and sloops, with nearly 9,000 sailors and 1,600 soldiers. Samuel Greig was in this squadron commanding the *Nadezhda Blagopoluchiia* (66). The Second Squadron, commanded by Counter-Admiral John Elphinstone, included four ships of line with support ships and nearly 4,000 sailors and 860 soldiers. Elphinstone was another Scot, born in Orkney, who had served in the Royal Navy at the capture of Quebec and the siege

---

4. TNA: FO SP 91/108, *St. Petersburg to Constantinople*, (October 1769).

of Havana. He entered Russian service in 1769 and returned to the Royal Navy in 1771.

A LIST of the RUSSIAN FLEET.

ADMIRAL ELPHINGSTON'S DIVISION.

Ships Names.	Captains Names.	Men	Guns
Swetafloff (admiral's ship)	Kmetefskoy	670	84
Netromena	Befchentioff	512	66
Saratoff	Stepanoff	512	66
Northern Eagle put back *	Jenjufnehoff		32
Nadifhda frigate	Palivinoff	212	32
Africa	Cleopin	212	32
Count Czernichew	Difhington		22
Count Panin	Bodie		18
Count Orloff	Arnold		18
St. Paul	Prefton		6

(Transport: Count Czernichew, Count Panin, Count Orloff, St. Paul)

ADMIRAL SPIRITDOFF'S DIVISION.

Ships	Captains	Men	Guns
St. Euftafie † (admiral's ship)	Krufe	512	66
Europa	Klokacheff	512	66
Januare	Borifoff	512	66
Trochfvatitelne, or the Three Saints	Roxburg	512	66
St. Nicholai	Policue, with a hundred Greeks on board		32

COUNT ORLOFF when he joined the Fleet near Paros.

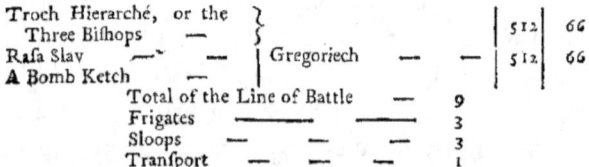

Ships	Captains	Men	Guns
Troch Hierarché, or the Three Bifhops		512	66
Rafa Slav	Gregoriech	512	66
A Bomb Ketch			

Total of the Line of Battle		9
Frigates		3
Sloops		3
Tranfport		1

The Veftal arm ship, with fome others, joined the Fleet a few days after the deftruction of the Turkifh.

Catherine had installed a Russian chargé d'affaires in Malta, and the fleet of the Order of St. John was used by Russian officers for training, along with the recruitment of naval officers. A plan was drawn up for a joint Russo-Maltese naval attack on the Greek mainland. However, the Mediterranean powers and the British were opposed to this. France remained the primary protector of the Order's neutrality, so the Order did not risk an open alliance with Russia. That came later, after the French Revolution, when Tsar Paul became the Order's Grand Master.[5] Food and stores had also been organised at Livorno, and Greek captains recruited.

---

5. T. Freller, *In search of a Mediterranean base: The order of St. John and Russia's great power plans during the rule of Tsar Peter the Great and Tsarina Catherine II* (January 2004, Journal of Early Modern History 8(1–2), pp. 3–30.

The First Squadron departed Kronstadt on 19 July 1769, taking a month just to reach Copenhagen. Half of the crew had no naval experience, and the sick list grew, with 332 having died by the time the squadron reached Minorca in December. The Second Squadron left Kronstadt on 9 October, but storm damage meant it spent December to January undertaking repairs at Portsmouth. Claude-Caroloman de Rulhiere described the British view, 'One can hardly describe the amusement with which the English viewed these ships of pinewood, their enormous heaviness in manoeuvring, their poops loaded with relics, the unhandiness of the sailors, the incredible dirtiness of their equipments, which was the veritable cause of a contagion that consumed them.'[6] Russian agents had hired merchant vessels in the region from Venice and other sources. They also encouraged privateers, also known as corsairs, mostly of Greek descent.

Orlov revolt

The First Squadron reached the Mani coast on 17 February 1770, at the harbour of Vitullo (Oitylo). Detachments of troops were landed and joined up with recruits for the Eastern Legion (led by Captain Barkov), totalling 1,200 volunteers, mainly from the Grigorakis clan. This force besieged some 3,000 Ottoman troops in Mistra, who agreed to surrender along with soldiers and civilians from the surrounding area. However, the Maniots massacred around 400 of the prisoners. A smaller Western Legion (led by Prince Dolgorukov) was also recruited with around 500 volunteers. This unit pressed inland, capturing Kalamata, Leontari, and Arkhadia, while the Russian fleet besieged coastal forts at Koroni and Methodi.

Mistra today (Author)

While these successes attracted recruits from the islands and Crete, their actions stiffened Ottoman resistance, with commanders unwilling to surrender. Fifteen thousand Albanian reinforcements arrived, and the eastern legion was heavily defeated at Tripolis. Barkov narrowly escaped back to the squadron, but the Eastern Legion was finished. The isolated Western Legion abandoned its operations and headed for Navarino, where Orlov was planning an assault on the bay that offered a better base for the fleet. Orlov blamed the failure of the land operations on the Maniots; they had an 'inclination toward servility and frivolity.'

---

6. B. Davies, *The Russo-Turkish War, 1768–1774*, (Bloomsbury, 2016), p. 154.

This was unfair, given the risks they took, and there was no recognition that Orlov had failed to support the revolt with adequate Russian troops. The Greeks thought the Russians were there to liberate them, when in fact, this was only a diversionary operation. The number of Greeks who took part in the rebellion is unclear. The Russians expected 100,000 to join the uprising, and Ottoman sources indicate that 50,000 to 80,000 participated. However, this seems to be an exaggeration, and not reflected in the modest number of troops the Ottomans deployed to crush the rebellion.[7]

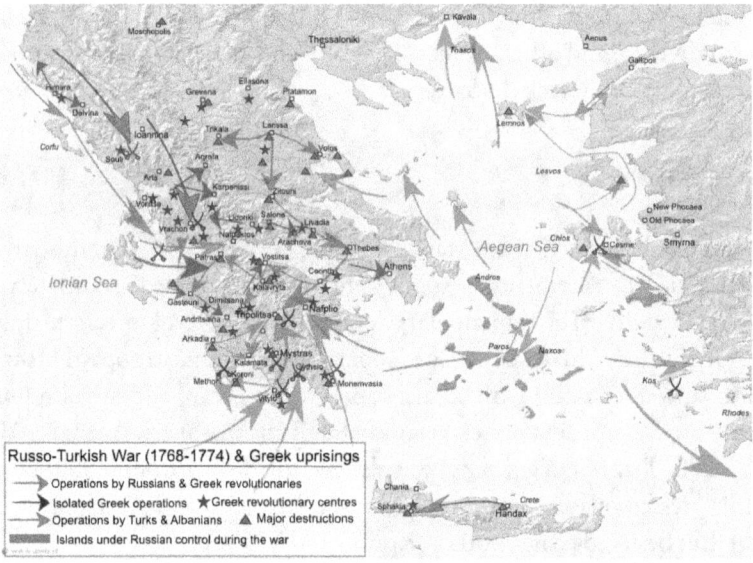

Map of Orlov Revolt. (Alexikoua, CC BY-SA 4.0)

Many Greek communities paid a high price when the Albanian troops took revenge for the earlier massacres. In Patras, nearly no one was left alive. Mystras was left in ruins, and the metropolitan bishop Ananias was executed. In the nine years following the revolt, around 20,000–30,000 local Greeks either died or left their homes. There was a similar story on Crete. A local Greek leader, Daskalogiannis, raised 2,000 men who started to kill local Muslims. This failed to rouse a broader revolt against Ottoman rule, and was quickly dispersed by the Ottoman garrison. On 24 March, Spiridov took three of his ships into Navarino Bay and landed 300 troops and ten heavy guns on the heights above the town. After a six-day bombardment, the walls were breached, and the Ottoman commander surrendered.

---

7. B. Gundogdu, *Ottoman Constructions of the Morea Rebellion*, 1770s (University of Toronto, 2012), p. 155.

Battle of Çeşme

The Second Squadron under Elphinstone arrived in the Aegean in May with four ships of the line and two frigates. He heard that a much larger Ottoman fleet of ten ships of the line, commanded by Ibrahim Hassan Bey Pasha, was in the Gulf of Nafplion in the eastern Peloponnese. He sailed to the gulf and attacked the Ottoman fleet, which overestimated the Russian strength and retired under the fortress guns. When Elphinstone attacked again, the Ottomans realised they outnumbered the Russians and counterattacked, driving the Russians off. They gave up the chase when they learned that Spiridov's First Squadron was approaching. The combined Russian fleet chased the Ottomans, skirmishing near the island of Spetses on 24 May. Relations between the two Russian commanders were poor, but Russian coordination partially improved when Orlov joined the fleet to take overall command. He had been forced to evacuate Navarino, marking the end of operations in the Morea.

Fortress at Nafplion today (Author)

On 5 July, the Ottoman fleet was spotted in the strait between the island of Chios and the mainland. This had expanded since Nafplion to sixteen ships of the line, six frigates, and as many as fifty small ships. The real commander was Hassan Bey Jezairli, an experienced Algerian admiral. He deployed his ships in a half-moon formation, which was a strong defensive position but gave the Russians the initiative, and they had the wind. They attacked in line ahead, with Spiridov's *Sv. Evstafi Plakidka* engaging Hassan Bey's flagship *Real-Mustafa*. The *Real-Mustafa* caught fire, and the flames reached the *Sv. Evstafi Plakidka* when its crew was boarding the enemy ship. Both ships had to be abandoned, and the rest of the Russian line was able to manoeuvre around to attack the rest of the Ottoman line. The Ottoman fleet feared the flames from the *Real-Mustafa* would spread to their other ships, so they cut their cables and withdrew into Çeşme Bay.

The Ottoman fleet was weakened but not destroyed. They positioned eight ships of the line across the bay, with the remaining vessels behind and shore batteries off both flanks. After a council of war, the Russians decided on a night attack on 6–7 July, which Grieg would lead with four ships of the line and a frigate. Once engaged, four fire ships would slip through the Ottoman line to spread fires to the reserve lines. Three of the fire ships couldn't get through, but the fourth contacted an Ottoman ship of the line, setting it on fire. By 02:00, the fire had spread across large sections of the Ottoman fleet, and by 04:00, crews abandoned their ships. The effect of the fire attack was astonishing. Fourteen ships of the line, six frigates, and fifty smaller vessels were destroyed, and 11,000 crew perished. Russian casualties totalled eleven killed.

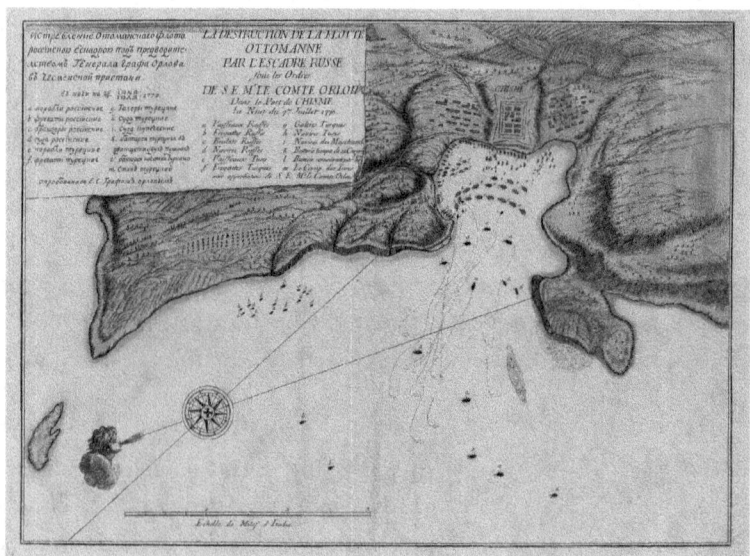

A period map of the Battle of Çheşme, June 1770

The victory at Çheşme gave the Russians complete control of the Aegean, and Elphinstone was sent with three ships of the line and two frigates to block the Dardanelles. This blocked vital grain shipments from Egypt to Constantinople. The Russian fleet was based at Lemnos, from where it unsuccessfully besieged the main fortress at Pelari. In December, the fleet was reinforced by the third squadron (Admiral I. N. Arf), comprising three ships of the line, one frigate, and 15 transports, which brought badly needed stores and additional troops, thereby increasing the infantry strength to 2,167. This enabled a closer blockade of the Dardanelles, although the failure to take Pelari allowed the Ottomans to land more troops on Lemnos. This forced the Russians to seek a new base at Port Auza on the island of Paros. From there, they established a federation of 14 islands, governed as a republic under Orlov's supervision. These islands supported the fleet and maintained a local militia. The Archipelagan Republic project was not fully formed when the war ended and the fleet withdrew. However, Davies argues it may have encouraged Catherine's later 'Greek Project.' It also strengthened Greek links with Russia, and under the Treaty of Küçük Kaynarca, Greek ships gained the right to sail under the Russian flag, having open access to the Black Sea and the Mediterranean. Russia also obtained the right to appoint consuls throughout the Empire, and most of these were Greeks.

For the remainder of the war, the Russian fleet patrolled the Aegean, seizing Ottoman shipping, countering piracy, and raiding the coast of Anatolia. They partially resolved their supply issues with captured Ottoman stores at Chalcis, Volos, Kavala, Makria Miti, and Lokroi. There was one significant naval battle off Patras on 6–8 November 1772. A Russian squadron, commanded by Captain Koniaev, consisting of two ships of the line, one frigate, and three sloops, defeated an Ottoman squadron of nine frigates and sixteen xebecs. Baron Tott argued that the Russians could have forced the Dardanelles before he strengthened the Ottoman defences, although this does not appear to be part of the Russian strategy. The fleet required continuous support from the Baltic Fleet, including a Fourth Squadron (Admiral Chichagov) in August 1772. Ten captured Ottoman frigates were subsequently refitted at Port Auza. When the fleet returned to the Baltic at the war's conclusion, the Russians had lost seven ships of the line to all causes and 4,516 men. However, for the period, it was a significant strategic achievement to maintain such a large fleet far from its home base, with untried commanders and sailors.

The Russians may also have been seeking naval support from Denmark. On 1 June 1773, the Treaty of Tsarskoye Selo was signed between the Russian Empire and Denmark-Norway. It transferred control of ducal Schleswig-Holstein to the Danish crown in return for Russian control of the County of Oldenburg and adjacent lands within the Holy Roman Empire. Denmark had a strong fleet, and the British ambassador to Paris reported that he believed a subsidiary treaty with Russia included them lending their ships. The ambassador didn't think the French would oppose a joint Danish-Russian fleet without Spanish support, but 'they will be very sorry to see them in the archipelago, and are anxious for Constantinople, which if properly attacked by such a fleet must fall.'[8] The war concluded before this prospect could materialise, but it makes an interesting what-if of history. Danish officers had already served in the Russian fleet. Rear Admiral Harf led a small squadron of reinforcements, with English transport ships, to the Mediterranean in 1770, with Catherine advising Orlov that 'the Danish officers who are undoubtedly recognized in their own homeland as being among the best, as well as a certain number of Danish sailors to supplement our insufficient numbers.'[9]

---

8. TNA: SP 78/288, *Ambassador letters to the Foreign Office*, (19 May, 1773).

9. Catherine to Orlov, 19 July 1770, *Catherine the Great: Selected Letters* (Oxford) p. 92.

Revolt in the Levant

In Egypt, Syria, and Palestine, the Ottoman Empire was administered differently from the Balkans and Anatolia. Relations with Constantinople were determined mainly by the families that gained power and held it on a hereditary basis. The 'Azms in Damascus intermittently controlled Damascus from 1730 into the early nineteenth century, based on a strong military, while maintaining good relations with the local elites. They kept the region in the Empire in return for a free hand in local affairs. The port of Acre was the base for a more independent ruler, Zahir al-'Umar al-Zaydani, who developed independent trade deals. However, in 1770 he was followed by Ahmad Pasha al-Jazzar ('the Butcher'), who maintained power by crushing independent power bases and was rewarded with further Ottoman appointments. Lebanon had a range of different groups who engaged in internecine warfare, until local leaders elected Bashir Shihab II as their leader, leaving Constantinople with no option other than to recognise him. This was a standard Ottoman response to insurrection; negotiation and incorporation were often preferable to expensive and challenging punitive expeditions.

Ali Bey, the Mamluk governor of Egypt, took the opportunity of the war to revolt against the Ottoman Empire. He had his name struck on local coins in 1769 (alongside the Sultan's emblem), effectively declaring Egypt's independence from Ottoman rule. In 1770, he gained control of the Hijaz. He sent an army into Syria, and in alliance with Pasha Dahir al-Umar, captured Damascus and Sidon in June 1771. However, Abu al-Dhahab, the commander of his troops in Syria, refused to continue the fight after an Ottoman agent stirred up mistrust between him and Ali Bey, and he returned to Egypt. Ali Bey lost power in 1772 and was killed in Cairo, probably in the following year.

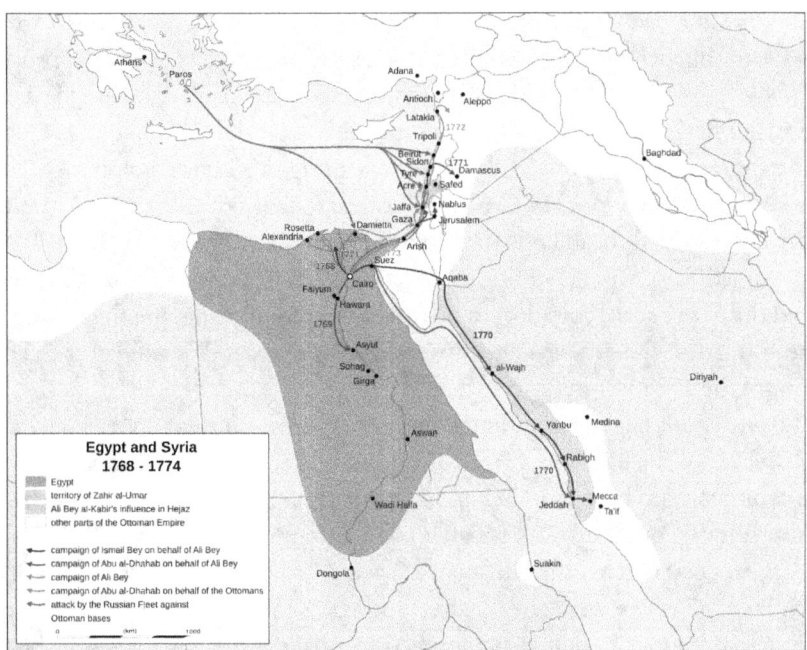

Egypt and Syria 1768-74 (Don-kun, Eric Gaba (Sting - fr:Sting), CC BY-SA 3.0)

When in Syria, they contacted Orlov to form an alliance with the Russian fleet. He sent Greek ships with Greek and Albanian mercenaries to Beirut in June 1772, sinking Ottoman ships and bombarding the town. A second squadron landed artillery, mercenaries, and some Russian officers in support of the revolt. In July 1773, a third expedition, comprising five Russian frigates and support ships (led by Captain Kozhukov and Major Voinovich), again bombarded Beirut and subsequently landed troops in September. They assisted in defeating an Ottoman force in the Bekaa Valley. Russian troops occupied Beirut until 2 January 1774.

The Black Sea after 1768

The victory in the 1768 war and the subsequent annexation of Crimea gave the Russian Navy almost total control of the northern Black Sea coast, with a string of new naval bases. The former Danube and Azov flotillas merged to form the Black Sea Fleet. However, this thirty-ship fleet was insufficient to control the Black Sea, and Catherine authorised the construction of twenty (64-gun) ships of the line in 1775. Potemkin, now a general-admiral, developed Kherson as a shipbuilding centre in 1778, although timber shortages meant only one ship of the line was built each year. Kherson did manage to construct around fifty-two frigates and smaller vessels.

Potemkin was aided by Admiral de Ribas, a Spaniard who had previously worked with Orlov. He helped build the ships, commanded the fleets, and even procured Potemkin's mistresses. It was Ribas who completed the construction of Odessa after Potemkin's death.

The Ottoman attempt to land in Crimea during the Tatar revolt in 1782 highlighted the need for a port in Crimea. The Tatar village of Akhtiar had a suitable deep water bay with headlands that could mount shore batteries. The new town was renamed Sevastopol (Greek for 'Venerable City'). Ushakov built a fortress to defend the town, and a squadron was based there, comprising one ship of the line, thirteen frigates, and ten smaller ships to patrol the coast. We will cover the naval actions of the 1787 war in chapter ten.

The Ottomans began rebuilding their fleet after the disaster at Chesme. Larger, 74-gun ships of the line were preferred to the smaller ships deployed in 1768. Ten were commissioned between 1772 and 1791. Earlier ships were described as frigates in most sources, but that was probably not an accurate description of these ships. True frigates first entered the Ottoman Navy in 1778 with the purchase of a British vessel. By 1787, there were ten frigates, although some of these were raze ships of the line that had kept their heavy lower deck artillery, enabling them to be used in the line of battle. Large bomb vessels, called bomb frigates (*bomba firkateym*), could also be confused with frigates. The emergence of the Russian Navy in the Mediterranean and the Black Sea led to a significant shift in Ottoman naval strategy, with a recognition that ships had to be able to compete in close-range firefights. However, these reforms had not been fully implemented by 1788.

Chapter Eleven

Peace and the Interregnum

Treaty of Küçük Kaynarca 1774

After just a few days of negotiation, the treaty was signed on 21 July 1774, in Küçük Kaynarca (now Kaynardzha, Bulgaria). It was signed for the Russians by Rumyantsev, and for the Ottomans by Muhsinzade Mehmed Pasha. One of the Ottoman signatories was Ahmed Resmi, a critic of the Tatars, who saw little to be gained from holding Crimea. A view reinforced by their conduct in the war— 'The Tatars were a mischief making, ill-omened people who had burdened the Sublime state from of old.'[1]

The treaty optimistically provided for a perpetual peace, and the vagueness of some provisions would form the basis for the resumption of the conflict in 1787. In return for abandoning their positions in Moldavia, Wallachia, and the Aegean, Russia gained Kabardia in the Caucasus, the ports of Azov, Kerch, and Yenikale on the Kerch Peninsula in the Crimea, and part of the Yedisan region between the Bug and Dnieper rivers at the mouth of the Dnieper. This latter territory included the port of Kherson, giving Russia two outlets to the Black Sea.

According to the Russians, the non-territorial provisions included the right to protect Christians in the Ottoman Empire and to intervene in Wallachia and Moldavia in the event of Ottoman misrule. However, this clause was not explicit and may be explained by the differences in the three languages (Russian, Ottoman, and Italian) used in the treaty. For example, the Russian text says that the Porte will 'take into consideration' the Russian representations; the Turkish text can be read to

---

1. A. Resmi, *A Chronicle of the 1768–1774 Russian-Ottoman War*, (Isis Press, 2011), p. 77.

mean simply that the Porte will 'receive' the representations. In 1775, the Russians published a French version of the treaty, which gave a Russian spin on the document, adding to the controversy. As other nations (including the British) translated the French into their languages, it became the widely accepted interpretation, with significant implications for the future.[2]

There was a contested provision to build an Orthodox church in Constantinople, although it was never built. The Russians also had the right to establish consuls throughout the Ottoman Empire and to allow the passage of ships through the Straits. The Tatars of the Crimea were recognised as politically independent, although in practice, they were under Russian influence. The sultan remained the religious leader of the Tatars as the Muslim caliph, the first time the powers of the Ottoman caliph were exercised outside of Ottoman borders and ratified by a European power. Finally, the Ottomans were to pay reparations totalling 4.5 million rubles.

Perhaps surprisingly, given their military victories in Moldavia and Wallachia, the Russians relinquished these territories in the peace treaty. Davies argues that this reflected the exhaustion of the Russian army and the problems faced by the Russians when administering these territories. The boyar factions made challenging demands on the Russians, and the area was devastated by plague and war damage.[3] Catherine, despite her grand manifesto offering liberation, was focusing more on Crimea. However, she would return to these issues in the 1780s.

Russian reforms

Once the Pugachev rebellion had been put down, Suvorov was sent to pacify the Bashkir tribes while Petr Panin restored order in the Volga region. This was achieved through a combination of incentives and punishments, with punitive expeditions and harsh reprisals complemented by famine relief.

Catherine also abolished the extra taxation levied to pay for the war, along with limited social reforms, such as pardoning fugitive serfs who returned to their masters, and ending corporal punishment without trial in the army. She recognised that poor local governance had contributed to the rebellion and, in 1775, introduced a new structure of 41 governorates (each with 300–400,000 taxpayers) divided into smaller districts (*uezd*). There was a clear separation of administrative, judicial, and

---

2. The interpretation of the treaty is considered in detail by R. Davison, *Russian Skill and Turkish Imbecility: The Treaty of Kuchuk Kainardji Reconsidered*, (Slavic Review 35, no. 3, 1976), pp. 463–83.

3. B. Davies, *The Russo-Turkish War*, 1768–1774, (Bloomsbury, 2016), p. 223.

fiscal functions, and each governor would report directly to the empress, with a seat on the Senate. Some governorates were paired under a governor-general, which somewhat undermined the reforms, and nearly all governors were military commanders. There were also limited forms of elected local government for the nobility in rural areas and the 'middle estate' in towns, who could advise the governor and run local services.

While the military value of Cossacks was recognised, the risk of revolt meant that their autonomy under elected atamans had to be curtailed. The Don Cossacks had an appointed ataman and a new council to manage military affairs, controlled by Potemkin as Governor-General of New Russia. They were organised into 500-strong regiments under appointed colonels and staff officers. The lands of the Zaporozhian Host had already been incorporated into New Russia, and with the Tatar threat from Crimea neutralised, their traditional border defence role was obsolete. Catherine therefore decided to abolish the Host and disperse its Cossacks, to open the territory to colonisation. Officers who swore allegiance to the empress were appointed to dragoon and hussar regiments, and many rank-and-file members were resettled in the Kuban and Astrakhan regions, with some fleeing to the Ottoman Empire. In the words of the order, 'The camp of these Cossacks, as the source of their unruliness, must be destroyed.'[4]

Potemkin embarked on a radical economic development of New Russia, almost doubling the population. The colonists had full Russian citizenship, received grants and loans, and were exempt from taxes and military service for a limited period. New Russia was divided into 70 districts, with 52 reserved for volunteers willing to take up military service (mainly as hussars) in return for tax exemptions. Foreign colonists were attracted with travel grants, loans, a 30-year tax exemption, and permanent exemption from military service. They were also granted freedom of religious expression and allowed to proselytise. The early colonists came from the Balkans, and later arrivals included Polish Jews, Danzig merchants, and 32,000 Greeks and Armenians from Crimea. Noblemen and industrialists could buy larger parcels of land to create estates. Potemkin founded new towns, including Kherson, Pavlograd, and Mariupol. The so-called 'Potemkin village,' a term used today to describe fake settlements or a facade, is largely a myth, propagated by his internal and external enemies. As Simon Sebag Montefiore concludes, 'Potemkin was a victim of his own overwhelming triumph. The "Potemkin Village" is itself one of history's biggest shams.'[5]

---

4. B. Davies, *The Russo-Turkish War, 1768–1774*, (Bloomsbury, 2016), p. 213.

5. S. Sebag Montefiore, *The Life of Potemkin*, (Phoenix Press, 2000), p. 383.

Ukraine also lost its special status as a borderland, with any resistance nullified by the sheer scale of Russian military garrisons in the region. Rumyantsev advised on a cautious integration into the new order with some compromises made to local autonomy, and he often appointed former Cossack commanders to posts in the new structure. However, Ukraine was incorporated into the new structure by 1779. Like Potemkin, as governor-general, Rumyantsev could countermand the orders of the governors and bypass the Senate, going directly to Catherine. He abolished the Cossack *polk* regiments, incorporating them into the regular army as carabiniers in 1783. Serfdom (although the word wasn't used) was effectively introduced in 1783, binding peasants to their estates. A large-scale flight ensued, with nearly 30,000 male peasants fleeing from Kiev province alone, mainly to New Russia.

Ottoman reforms

Shortly before his death in 1774, Sultan Mustafa III composed this short poem describing the state of the Empire:
The world is turning upside down, with no hope for better during our reign,
Wicked fate has delivered the state into the hands of despicable men,
Our bureaucrats are villains, who prowl through the streets of Constantinople,
We can do nothing but beg God for mercy.[6]

His brother, Abdul Hamid I, succeeded him. The new sultan had spent most of his life in seclusion in the palace, not expecting to become sultan. However, he appeared to grasp the need for reform, with Shaw saying, 'He left his mark as one of the strongest reforming sultans of the eighteenth century'—arguably not a high bar.[7] His approach was to adopt traditionalistic reform, while introducing military technologies from the European armies. He was helped by two reforming grand viziers, Kara Vezir Seyyit Mehmet Pasha (1779–1781) and Halil Hamit Pasha (1782–1785).

Ahmed Resmi wrote a report on the need for reform based on the experience of the 1769 campaign. The focus was on the failure in the supply system, and he made thirteen recommendations, including discipline on the march route, supply of horses, the poor quality of Anatolian troops ('filthy horde of thieves and vagabonds'), and militias generally. He also recommended expelling the camp followers, which exceeded 20,000, reducing the retainers of officers, improving the

---

6. B. Mugnai, *The Ottoman Army of the Napoleonic Wars*, (Helion, 2022), p. 11.

7. S. Shaw, *History of the Ottoman Empire and Modern Turkey, Volume 1* (Cambridge, 1976), p. 251.

quality of supplies, and providing better treatment for pack animals. The most challenging task was reforming the Janissaries, which would not be achieved for a generation. It was a rare document in Ottoman culture, and sadly for the Empire, very little was implemented until the next century.

Abdul Hamid was the first sultan to bring in large numbers of foreign advisors without requiring them to adopt Ottoman dress or convert to Islam. The most influential was Baron Francois de Tott, a Hungarian who had fled to France after the Rakoczi revolt. He served in the French artillery and came with the French ambassador to the Porte in 1755. After his embassy to Crimea in 1767, he was hired to create a modern artillery corps. During the 1768 war, he built new defences for the Dardanelles and devised a pontoon system for river crossings. In 1774, he established the Rapid-Fire (*Süratçi*) Artillery Corps, assisted by a Scottish officer named Campbell and a Frenchman, Aubert. He also built a new cannon foundry and started a mathematics school. Campbell and Aubert continued the corps when de Tott returned to France in 1776. A modern approach to fortifications was still balanced with the traditional. When Tott started to rebuild the castles defending entry to the Black Sea, the grand vizier consulted the chief astrologer over the exact time the first stone should be laid.[8]

The Ottoman Navy was reformed under the leadership of Gazi Hasan Pasha, a survivor of the Battle of Chesma, which had wiped out the old naval establishment. He built new shipyards, appointing French naval engineers to design ships similar to those of the French and British navies, i.e. with a lighter draft and greater manoeuvrability. He also professionalised the training of officers and sailors, instituting barracks and the Naval Engineering School. By 1784, the fleet had twenty-two new ships of the line and fifteen frigates. He was less successful in overcoming the corruption in the appointment of new naval officers, and conditions aboard ships lacked the discipline he sought to impose.

In the Ottoman principalities of Wallachia and Moldavia, the new rulers (Hospodar) were Orthodox Christians and careful not to provoke unrest or give the Russians any excuse to intervene under the treaty provisions. Taxes were kept stable, and confiscated lands were largely returned to monasteries and boyars. In Wallachia, tax laws were simplified, and officials were paid salaries to reduce corruption. The region benefited from an economic revival, which boosted revenues without having to increase the rate of taxation. However, in the 1780s, the new Russian consuls in the region used their position to build pro-Russian networks amongst the boyars and churchmen, even winning support from hospodars in Moldavia. The Russian strategy may have been influenced by growing Austrian influence in the Balkans.

---

8. G. Goodwin, *The Janissaries*, (Saqi Books, 1994), p. 198.

The Ottomans also faced decentralisation with the growing power of the provincial *ayans*. These warlords had played a crucial role in the 1768 war, and Balkan leaders such as Ali Pasha of Janina and Osman Pazvantoglu of Vidin expanded their territories and acted independently of the government in Constantinople. There were similar, if not stronger, ayans in Anatolia and the Middle East, with the Mamluks taking effective control of Egypt. The sultan was forced to appoint ayans into official positions or bribe them to carry out his policies. The occasional military expeditions to subdue them often led to the troops defecting to the ayans, who offered better pay and conditions. The loss of tax revenue weakened the Ottoman treasury, leaving major cities short of food. Russia was not the only external threat. A revitalised Iran under the Zand Dynasty pursued an aggressive foreign policy against the Ottomans, until a nominal Ottoman pasha restored control.

The Janissaries and Sipahis managed to recover most of their strength but resisted reform, aided by conservative elements in the establishment. Minor changes were made during a crisis, but once it eased, business returned to normal. The reforming Grand Vizier Halil Hamit did recognise the need for reform among the older corps. Inspectors went out to the provinces to ensure sipahis lived on their assigned lands and received proper training, while also rooting out corruption. Janissaries who refused to train were dismissed, and the children of Janissaries were only allowed to enlist if they demonstrated the necessary skills. He dismissed two-thirds of the Janissaries on the rolls and used the money saved to raise salaries for the rest, thus avoiding a revolt. He also sent French engineers to improve the border fortresses and made sure they were adequately supplied. However, his success bred enemies who managed to persuade the sultan that he was plotting to replace him with his nephew, Selim, who may have been more receptive to reform. Halil Hamit was dismissed and then executed in April 1785.

Greek Project

Catherine's Greek Project was developed between 1779 and 1782, renewing a vision of a restored Byzantine Empire after the Ottoman Empire was partitioned, in a manner similar to Poland's partition. Potemkin, an ardent Hellenophile with a classical education, encouraged Catherine, persuading her to prioritise Greek over Latin in the education of Catherine's grandsons. This vision had roots going back to Peter the Great and the 1736 war. For Potemkin, persuading Catherine to overthrow the Islamic yoke had a strong religious element: Russia as the protectorate of all ancestral Orthodox lands. Voltaire also encouraged Catherine in his letters during the 1768 war, which was reflected in Catherine's instructions to Orlov during his Mediterranean expedition. Voltaire was so carried away with Greek models that he recommended the use of chariots, 'which, in his opinion, would be particularly effective on the steppes of the Black Sea area.'[9] Catherine had to bring him back to earth with, 'My military men claim, Sir, that, now that cannons have been invented, Solomon's twelve thousand chariots are of little use alongside a good artillery battery.'[10] While some historians dismiss the Greek Project as an idealistic fantasy, others argue it was a genuine geopolitical strategy.[11] Ragsdale contends that the limited archival sources reflect the level of secrecy Catherine insisted on.

In the 1780 *Notes on Political Affairs*, the Greek Project envisioned another war against the Ottomans, in which Russia and Austria would partition the Ottoman Empire, with Austria taking large parts of the western Balkans and Russia controlling lands in the east. A new kingdom of Dacia would be formed, incorporating Wallachia and Moldavia, to be ruled by Potemkin. Greece and Bulgaria would be joined to create a new empire based on Constantinople, ruled by Catherine's grandson, Konstantin Pavlovich. Catherine confided to a visitor to her court that her aim was 'to chase the Turks out of Europe and enthrone herself in Byzantium.'[12] Catherine's big idea was that Europe's political leadership should consist of two empires: that of the Viennese, heir to Rome, and that of Petersburg, heir to Constantinople.

The project took practical steps in the 1780 summit between Catherine and Austria's Joseph II. This was something of a détente, as Joseph and his mother Maria Theresa had previously regarded Catherine as a nymphomaniacal regicide.[13] Despite this, Joseph and Catherine appeared to get on well, with Catherine recalling their meeting as 'the best and most memorable day of my life.' They had similar responsibilities as autocrats running massive and disparate empires, and they had much in common: simple personal lifestyles, liberal views (of a sort), and widely read. Joseph reciprocated the admiration, saying, 'Her spirit, her high mindedness, her bravery, her pleasing conversation have to be experienced to be appreciated.' However, he was less impressed with her 'Greek Project,' as she repeatedly raised it in their discussions. His mother, Maria Theresa, had previously commented scathingly on the idea of a partition of the Ottoman Empire: 'What would we gain in pushing our conquests to Constantinople? Unwholesome (*malsaines*) provinces, barbarous (*sans culture*), depopulated, or inhabited by perfidious or ill-intentioned

---

9. A. Zorin, *By Fables Alone*, (Academic Studies Press, 2014), p. 35.

10. Catherine to Voltaire, 14 July 1769, *Catherine the Great: Selected Letters* (Oxford), pp. 77–78).

11. E. Bryant, *A Third Rome? Catherine the Great's "Greek Project"*, (The Crimson Historical Review, Vol V, No. 1, 2022), pp. 54–63.

12. C. Erickson, *Great Catherine*, (Simon & Schuster, 1994), p. 332.

13. S. Montefiore, *Prince of Princes: The Life of Potemkin*, (Phoenix Press, 2000), p. 221.

Greeks more capable of exhausting than of augmenting the power of my Monarchy.'[14]

This summit led to a Russo-Austrian alliance against the Ottomans, and the Russians abandoned Prussia and the northern strategy in favour of expansion to the south. Frederick the Great recognised the threat and sent his heir, Frederick William, to Russia to meet Catherine. However, Catherine was not impressed with the socially limited prince, nicknaming him 'Fat Gu'. The Prussophile Grand Duke Paul did welcome the prince, but that only further alienated him from Catherine and Potemkin.

After 1774, there was large-scale Greek emigration to the Russian Empire, and the Russian consuls continued to develop networks in Greece. However, Catherine appears to have realised that the project would require a war on a scale that even the Russians and Austrians combined would struggle to sustain financially. Austria was also less interested in destroying the Ottoman Empire and would face its own challenges in the west when the French Revolution erupted in 1789. While the war did not deliver the project, it did weaken the Porte and boost Russia's image in the Balkans. Catherine never abandoned her project, but merely postponed it when faced with difficulty. It did end with her death, as her successor, Paul, was vehemently against the Greek Project.

Britain and the conflict

The Russo-Ottoman wars may appear to have been a remote consideration for Britain and its relationships with Russia and the Ottoman Empire. Britain had cordial relationships with Russia dating back to the early days of Muscovy, primarily centred on trade. A limited preliminary treaty was agreed upon in 1755 (lasting four years), involving British subsidies in return for 55,000 Russian troops on their Livonian border, to work with a Royal Navy squadron in case of war.[15]

The isolation of Britain in Europe and Russia's military potential during the Seven Years' War helped to recommend such an alliance in London. Britain's naval power and her wealth, with possible subsidies, were strong attractions to Catherine and her ministers. France's support for the Ottomans naturally gravitated Britain into support for Russia, helped by Catherine's hostility to France. Pitt, writing to Lord Shelburne in 1773, said, 'Your Lordship knows quite well that I am quite a Russ; I trust the Ottoman Empire will pull down the House of Bourbon in

---

14. H. Ragsdale, *Evaluating the Traditions of Russian Aggression: Catherine II and the Greek Project*, (The Slavonic and East European Review, Vol. 66, No. 1, Jan., 1988), pp. 91–117.

15. TNA: SP 113/132, *Russia Treaty provisions*, (September 1755).

its fall.'[16] However, British support didn't go as far as what became known as the 'Turkish Clause', an undertaking by Britain that a Turkish attack on Russia should rank as a *casus foederis* under the new treaty of alliance.[17] This marked the beginning of a slow decline in British-Russian relations during the 1768 war.

In Constantinople, the British and Russian ambassadors worked closely together, including sharing documents. The British ambassador, Sir John Murray, shared his intelligence on Ottoman troop movements and logistics, which was passed to London in his dispatches.[18] However, he may well have overstated the position when he reported to London that 'M. Obreskov's credit at the Porte is great; he is indefatigable in his endeavours.' The Russian ambassador was imprisoned shortly afterwards. After the war broke out, Murray shared intelligence with Lord Cathcart, the British ambassador to St. Petersburg.[19]

Britain had aided the Russian naval campaign in the Mediterranean during the 1768 war. Orlov's fleet would have struggled to even reach the Mediterranean from the Baltic without help from the Royal Navy. One of the Russian squadrons was commanded by a Royal Navy officer, John Elphinston. The Greek Project would require further assistance from Britain, and Potemkin sought a Russian naval base on Minorca. Catherine was less convinced, pointing to the distances involved and the fleet's dependency on Britain, which in any case soon lost the island. In 1783, Britain supported Catherine in her annexation of Crimea. Despite this naval assistance, Britain saw its role as a mediator, a position not reciprocated by either of the combatants, at least at the war's outbreak, and Prussia was also offering to play this role. Naval assistance to the Russians was highlighted by the French, ending any prospect of the British being viewed as a neutral party by the Ottomans. By 1773, the French were beginning to fit out a squadron in Toulon to challenge the Russians.

In an early manifestation of what would become the 'Great Game' between Britain and Russia, Potemkin was pursuing a Persian Project that would incorporate the Orthodox Georgians into the Russian Empire. He persuaded Catherine to authorise a modest expedition to establish a trading post in Persia, led by Count Voinovich, a Dalmatian sailor. Persia was in some disarray at the time, and one of the factions led by Aga-Mohommed initially welcomed this initiative. However,

---

16. J. Marriot, *Anglo-Russian Relations 1689-1943*, (Methuen, 1944), p. 51.

17. M. Anderson, *Great Britain and the Russo-Turkish War of 1768-74*, (The English Historical Review, Volume LXIX, Issue CCLXX, January 1954), pp. 40-41.

18. The National Archives: FO SP110/86, *Sir John Murray to Foreign Office*.

19. TNA: FO SP 91/108, *St. Petersburg letters*, (from 1768).

Voinovich lacked diplomatic skills, and his modest force of three frigates and 650 men did not impress the Persians. They surrounded the Russians and gave them the choice of losing their heads or evacuating. They wisely chose the latter, and Potemkin's vision came to nothing.

However, his Georgian plans made some progress when King Hercules offered his kingdom to Russia in the Treaty of Georgievsk on 24 July 1783.

Intelligence reports from the British Ambassador to the Foreign Office were encrypted.(TNA: SP97/44)

In 1785, Potemkin persuaded Catherine to take British convicts who had not been transported to their colonies due to the American War of Independence. However, Potemkin's rival Vorontsov, who was serving as the Russian ambassador to Britain, persuaded her against the project. We should remember that transportation was a punishment for relatively minor crimes by modern standards. Therefore, many of these convicts would possess valuable skills, and Russia had a long history of utilising criminals to settle inhospitable areas, such as Siberia. Even the modern Russian state emptied its prisons to provide 'cannon fodder' for the invasion of Ukraine. However, Potemkin drew the line at taking American loyalists after the revolution, fearing they might be the descendants of Cromwellian ideas!

Potemkin was something of an Anglophile and recruited an eclectic mix of British advisors, with mixed success. The gardener William Gould created formal gardens throughout the region with a staff that numbered in the hundreds. He most famously employed Samuel Bentham (brother of the philosopher Jeremy Bentham, who also spent time in Russia) as a shipbuilder, inventor, and engineer. Bentham's inventions included an amphibious vessel and an articulated barge built for Catherine the Great, as well as the first Panopticon (circular prison). He eventually assumed complete responsibility for Potemkin's factories and workshops. After his return to Britain, Bentham was appointed Inspector General of Naval Works in 1796, responsible for maintaining and improving the Royal dockyards.

The Eastern Question was a dominant foreign policy issue for Britain in the late nineteenth century, but its roots were from much earlier. Some historians date it from 1791, when the government proposed to increase naval strength to resist Russian aggression against the Ottoman Empire.[20] At the start of the 1787 war, Britain was relaxed about Russia expanding into Ottoman territory, with Prime

---

20. A. Cunningham, *Anglo-Ottoman Encounters in the Age of Revolution*, (Frank Cass, 1993), p. 1.

Minister Pitt announcing Britain's 'perfect neutrality' to the Russian ambassador. Britain's primary commercial interest was in the eastern Mediterranean, with the Levant Company even paying the salary of the British ambassador to Constantinople (Robert Ainslie), a post regarded as second-tier in the Foreign Office pecking order. The ambassador's letters are dominated by commercial issues in the Levant.[21] Ainslie discouraged British contractors from supplying the Ottoman army and looked after Russian embassy officials and their families, after their ambassador was imprisoned.[22]

The British government had an alliance with Prussia, which tried to engage Britain in its eastern plans. However, Britain's interest in the alliance was in the Low Countries, not the Eastern Question. They also rejected Catherine's approach when she outlined her war aims in 1788, and refused to promote them in Constantinople. Catherine also rebuffed British and Prussian attempts at mediation. This led to what became known as the 'Ochakov Debates' in parliament over Britain's short-lived ultimatum to Russia, with Pitt insisting that the Russian capture of the fortress had profound implications for Britain. This was despite advice from a Dutch admiral, who was familiar with the area, that the fort didn't even dominate the estuary, let alone the wider Black Sea region. The Whig opposition leader (Fox), well informed by the Russians, ambushed the government in the House of Commons, and a climbdown followed. He argued that the cost of a fleet over an issue with minimal British interest was folly. Trade with Russia was worth nearly £3 million, with British merchant ships dominating the trade. The Whigs argued that the Ottoman Empire was of no consequence to Great Britain, and Ochakov wasn't even critical to Ottoman security. Pitt offered only a half-hearted defence of the policy, privately only emphasising the need to support Prussia, during the emerging French Revolution. However, others highlighted the risks of Russian expansionism, with Lord Mulgrave saying, 'Ever since she emerged from barbarism, about two hundred years ago, [Russia] had been pursuing one regular scheme of ambition to extend her conquests far and wide.'[23]

Catherine had made plans to engage privateers to attack British ships if Britain declared war, using John Paul Jones, although she was sceptical about threatening India. She wrote to Baron Grimm, 'For us to take all their ships we can with our

---

21. TNA: FO SP110/87, *Sir John Murray to Foreign Office*.

22. TNA: FO SP 97/44, *Sir John Murray to Foreign Office*.

23. A. Cunningham, *Anglo-Ottoman Encounters in the Age of Revolution*, (Frank Cass, 1993), p. 26.

privateers; then they would end the war very quickly. As to India, it is so far away that before anyone can get there, peace will be made.'[24]

Annexation of Crimea

In Crimea, Khan Devlet Giray continued his revolt after the treaty was signed. The tribes of the Kuban steppe were not bound by the treaty, and refused to accept the new Crimean Khanate's protectorate over them. This enabled Devlet Giray to land in Crimea, and the new khan, Sahip Giray, fled. The Ottomans refused to abandon the treaty provisions regarding an independent Crimea or assist Devlet in ejecting the Russians. The Russians took a pragmatic decision to recognise him, while supporting the young Shahin Giray, with funds and troops, in his government of the Nogais in the Kuban as a possible future replacement.

Devlet managed to consolidate his position in Crimea, winning support from the nobles. The Ottomans agreed to place him under their protection, but sent no troops, other than those still at Taman (which should have been evacuated under the treaty) and Ochakov. The Russians decided to strengthen their garrisons in the region, reinforced Shanin's army, and trained some units in the European manner. On 21 November 1776, the Russian General Prozorovskii led an incursion into Crimea with 15,000 troops, citing the Ottoman failure to evacuate Taman as justification. Shanin's army failed to capture Taman, suffering heavy losses. However, the peace party in Constantinople was driving Ottoman policy, and they pressed Devlet to abdicate, allowing Shahin to assume power in April 1777.

Shanin Giray introduced a more centralised and autocratic regime in Crimea. This included a new local administration, progressive taxation, and land reform. He created a regular 'New Model' army, 20,000 strong, trained and equipped in the European manner. However, the reforms alienated many Muslim Tatars, who resented the introduction of Christian colonists and the European advisors at the khan's court. A revolt broke out, and the khan's palace was ransacked and his vizier killed. General Prozorovskii had to intervene to save the khan. Greek colonists burned Tatar villages along the coast, killing hundreds. The Ottoman sultan declared Shanin an apostate and sent 7,000 troops and a fleet of 100 ships to intervene. However, the Russians managed to prevent this force from landing, and the peace party again persuaded the sultan to sign the Aynalıkavak Convention in January 1779, which regulated the withdrawal of all foreign troops from Crimea. Over 30,000 Greek colonists, fearing reprisals, also evacuated to Azov and along the

---

24. Catherine to Baron Grimm (16 September, 1791), in F. Golder, *John Paul Jones in Russia*, (Doubleday, 1927), p. 218.

banks of the River Don. This was encouraged by Potemkin because the Christians of Crimea were wealthy craftsmen or merchants, and paid considerable taxes. An exodus of Christians would not only leave Shanin Giray with the Tatar element of his subjects, who were antagonistic towards his policies, but it would also deal a significant blow to the Khanate's economy.

Shahin yet again overreached himself with a campaign in the North Caucasus, which encouraged a new revolt in Crimea. The Russians had to intervene again to save him. Potemkin urged Catherine to abandon Shahin and annexe Crimea to the Empire. He argued that direct rule would address Shahin's oppressive administration and grant Russia control of the Black Sea coast. In a stream of imperialistic rhetoric, he exclaimed to Catherine, 'Imagine the Crimea is yours and the wart on your nose is no more. Gracious Lady...You are obliged to raise Russian glory!...Russia needs paradise.'[25] Catherine's personal secretary, A.A. Bezborodko, saw the annexation of Crimea as an integral part of achieving the ultimate goal of taking Constantinople.

On 8 April 1783, Catherine announced the annexation of Crimea, the Taman peninsula, and the right bank of the Kuban River to the Empire. This brought the Russians directly into confrontation with the Ottomans in the Caucasus, bypassing intermediaries. While the Ottomans had breached the treaty provisions themselves, this action would typically have led to a declaration of war. However, the French and British, preoccupied with the American War of Independence, urged restraint. The grand vizier, Halil Hamid Pasha, believed the army and fleet were not strong enough to retake Crimea, and he feared Austrian intervention in the Balkans. He also understood that there simply weren't the financial resources to pay for a new war. The treasury advised that fifteen million *kurus* (silver pieces) were needed to finance the war, the equivalent of the treasury's total annual revenue. The grand admiral estimated the costs of building a battle fleet at 6–7.5 million *kurus*[26]. Therefore, a convention was agreed on 9 January 1784, acknowledging the annexation.

The new Russian governor, Otto von Igel'strom, slowly implemented reforms and was careful to respect Muslim traditions. By putting the religious establishment on Russian salaries and controlling appointments, Russia was also able to reduce the Sultan's influence in Crimea on religious issues. Native military units were raised using volunteers rather than conscription into the Russian army, including six new regular infantry regiments. More than three hundred Tatar nobles were co-opted into the Russian nobility, and the peasants on their estates were effectively bound

---

25. S. Montefiore, *Prince of Princes: The Life of Potemkin*, (Phoenix Press, 2000), p. 249.

26. G. Agoston, J. Black ed., *European Warfare, 1453–1815*, (Macmillan, 1999), *Ottoman Warfare in Europe 1453–1826*, p. 143.

to the land, although not formally as serfs. Many Tatars had already emigrated from Crimea in the 1768 war and subsequent revolts. The Greek colonists returned, along with others from Greece. Russian colonists and Cossacks were also settled in Crimea, which significantly changed the ethnic makeup of the region. Ports were developed at Simferopol, Balaklava, and Sevastopol (Greek names reflecting Potemkin's Greek Project), shifting maritime trade westwards, with links to a new port in Ukraine based on the small Ottoman fort of Haji-bey, renamed Odessa.

By 1793, Potemkin's Ekaterinoslav Viceroyalty reached a population of 819,731, expanding commercial farming at a rate unheard of until the railroad in North America helped develop the American Midwest or the Canadian prairies. There were some revolts. The Nogais were considered a security risk, and Potemkin ordered Suvorov to forcibly move them further away from Ottoman agitators. Many revolted, and it took two campaigns to pacify them. Cossacks were resettled along a new line of forts, known as the Mozdok Line. These defences disrupted traditional Kabardian grazing lands, and they frequently attacked the line. In 1785, the first of what would become a regular feature of Russian colonial existence occurred: a Chechen revolt led by Al-Mansur. This guerrilla war continued until 1794, despite numerous Russian punitive expeditions into the mountains and forests of the region. The Comte de Damas' observations of Potemkin's work were typical of Western observers. 'He would move a guberniya (province), demolish a town with a view to building it somewhere else, form a new colony or a new industrial centre, and change the administration of a province, all in a spare half hour before giving his whole attention to the arrangement of a ball or fete.'[27]

In 1787, Catherine set out on a six-month, six-thousand-kilometre tour of Ukraine, New Russia, and Crimea. A grand triumphal tour of inspection, of which she wrote, 'I am very happy to have seen it all with my own eyes....This land is an earthly paradise.' It was also a curated piece of political theatre, with a large tail of foreign dignitaries to be entertained along the route. In a flotilla of eighty boats, seven new galleys had been built for the journey down the Dnieper, each with its own staff and twelve musicians, christened 'Cleopatra's fleet'. Emperor Joseph also joined the party for a period in Crimea, sleeping in giant tents, and was entertained by Potemkin. At Sevastopol, Potemkin organised a massive parade with 10,000 troops, dressed in their traditional regional costumes, along with the fleet. These included a Greek battalion of warrior women. The troops shouted, 'Long live the Empress of Pontus Euxinus!'

It provoked the Ottomans, probably as it was intended to do, along with Russian mischief in the Balkans and the Caucasus. The Russians had cut the Ottoman port of Ochakov from its salt trade, while Ottoman subjects seized a Russian ship off

---

27. S. Montefiore, *Prince of Princes: The Life of Potemkin*, (Phoenix Press, 2000), p. 263.

Algiers. The reformist group, which probably still included Ahmed Resmi, argued for adherence to the 1774 treaty. However, the conservatives were revitalised by the Crimean issue and gained support from Tatar exiles in Constantinople. The new grand vizier, Koca Yusef Pasha, was preparing for war and prevailed over the peace party led by the experienced and cautious Grand Admiral Gazi Hasan Pasha.[28]

---

28. Gazi Hasan Pasha was the son of a Georgian Orthodox servant on the Barbary Coast. Having survived Chesme, he put down a revolt in Egypt and was nicknamed the 'Crocodile of Sea Battles'. According to a British visitor in 1786, he was always accompanied by a pet lion who that lay down at his command.

Chapter Twelve

War Resumes, 1787–92

When the Ottomans demanded that the Russians evacuate Crimea and give up their ports on the Black Sea, Russia declared war on 19 August 1787. The Ottomans imprisoned the Russian ambassador, Yakov Bulgakov, in their traditional way of declaring war. Being an ambassador to the Porte was not an easy posting.

Russia had to retain significant forces in the north, due to the threat of war with Sweden and possibly Britain. In the south, three armies were planned to be ready for the 1788 campaign season. Potemkin's Ekaterinoslav Army of 75,000 men and 200 guns on the Dniester; Rumyantsev's Ukrainian Army of 40,000 men and 96 guns; and Tekelli's (Tokeli) Crimean Army of 30,000 men. Rumyantsev would be semi-retired by 1789, replaced by Nikolai Repnin, with Potemkin in overall command.

The Ottomans mobilised around 200,000 men under the command of Grand Vizier Koca Yusuf Pasha. However, troops from Wallachia, Serbia, and Bosnia had to be retained to defend and raid Austrian territories. They also sent most of their fleet to the Black Sea, commanded by Gazi Hasan.

Battle of Kinburn, 12 October 1787

The Ottoman offensive began at Kinburn (in modern Ukraine), opposite the Ottoman fortress at Ochakov (Özi), on a spit of land that defended the approach to the Dnieper River and the port of Kherson. Suvorov commanded the Russian garrison, which included over 300 guns and 1,500 infantry. He had a further mobile corps of around 2,500 infantry and light cavalry, 38 guns, and 1,500 Cossacks. The infantry was drawn from the Orel, Schisselburg, Kozlov, and Murmon regiments, with cavalry from the Marioupol and Pavlograd Hussar regiments. The St. Petersburg Dragoon Regiment and Don Cossacks arrived at the end of the battle. Two Russian frigates and four galleys, part of Admiral Mordvinov's squadron, were sent to support the garrison. The Ottoman force of over 5,000 men was commanded by Serben-Geşti-Eyyub-Ağa, supported by three ships of the line, four frigates, four bomb vessels, and 14 gunboats. They were advised by a French officer, André Lafitte-Clave, whom the Ottomans sent to prepare the defences of Ochakov in April 1787.

The Ottoman force arrived on 25 September 1787 and opened fire on the Russian gun emplacements. The Russian ships managed to drive off the Ottoman gunboats, but the fleet returned on 11 October and landed an assault force under cover of a fleet bombardment the following morning. Following the usual Ottoman practice, these troops dug trenches and moved slowly towards Kinburn. Suvorov sent two regiments on a sortie, which reached the trenches but were forced back under shelling from the Ottoman fleet, and after their commander was wounded. Suvorov personally led the second sortie, but it also failed when he was wounded, and he was saved only through the courage of a grenadier from the Schlisselburg Grenadier Regiment. At 4:00 pm, Russian reinforcements arrived, and Suvorov launched another attack, this time with his Cossacks infiltrating the Ottoman position from the rear.

Grenadier Novikov saves Suvorov at Kinburn (Stasulevich)

This forced them back to the coast, where the Ottoman fleet could not provide effective fire support. The Russian artillery decimated the Ottoman infantry on the beaches. At night, the Ottomans evacuated the approximately 600 survivors. The Russians lost 250 dead and 750 wounded. Lafitte-Clavé claimed the attack would have been successful if the Janissaries had followed his plan and the troops had been more disciplined. He was critical of the practice of rewarding soldiers for capturing men and equipment because they abandoned the fight: 'I saw several of them approach the commander with seven or eight heads, and myself saved one of their captives by expressing the need to extract information from him.'[1]

On the Moldavian front, the Russian army, led by Ivan Saltykov, captured Khotyn and Iaşi (Jassy) in 1788, with support from an Austrian corps led by Prince Josias of Coburg.

---

1. V. Aksan, *Ottoman Wars 1700–1870*, (Pearson, 2007), p. 162.

Siege of Ochakov (Özi), May–December 1788

Having held on to Kinburn, the Russian forces in Ukraine, numbering some 40,000 and led by Potemkin and Suvorov, advanced on the major Ottoman fortress of Ochakov in May 1788. Located at the mouth of the Dnieper, the fortress defended access to the river and was difficult to attack from land. The defences had been strengthened by a French engineer, Lafite, with a double ditch and six bastions. It had been successfully defended before, notably during the 1736–39 war, and was crucial if the Ottomans were going to recover the Crimea. The two Russian commanders disagreed on strategy. Suvorov wanted to storm the fortress, while Potemkin favoured a siege. Potemkin surrounded the city and began a formal siege and bombardment. Most sources indicate that the Ottoman garrison consisted of around 20,000 men, commanded by Hüseyin Pasha. However, captured Ottoman officers in the naval actions indicated, 'We learn from the Prisoners of Mark that there are eight thousand soldiers in the Fortress, who, they say, are not well disciplined.'[2]

The Ottomans brought a mixed fleet to the area on 31 May, commanded by Gazi Hasan Pasha. It probably consisted of 12 small ships of the line, 13 frigates and xebecs, two bomb vessels, two galleys, ten gunboats, and six fireships. The Russians had a smaller fleet comprising three small ships of the line (40 guns), six frigates (24–34 guns) and five smaller vessels, as well as a gunboat flotilla commanded by Prince Charles of Nassau-Siegen[3] and John Paul Jones. Potemkin made both of them rear admirals, and their objective was to blockade the port, although they squabbled and Potemkin had to referee their disputes. The shallow water in the Liman Estuary meant neither side could deploy their heavy ships; this was to be a clash of galleys and smaller vessels.

On 18 June, five Turkish galleys and 36 small craft attacked the inshore end of the Russian line, where the Russians had only six galleys, four barges, and four double-sloops to oppose them. Ottoman reinforcements arrived at 10:00 am, but Nassau-Siegen and Jones had advanced the offshore ends to bring their whole force into action. The Ottomans withdrew after three of their vessels were blown up.

---

2. Letter, Paul Jones to Potemkin (20 June, 1788) in F. Golder, *John Paul Jones in Russia*, (Doubleday, 1927), p. 174.

3. Prince (his right to the title was contested) Charles of Nassau-Siegen was a French-born adventurer who attached himself to Prince Potemkin. He had previous experience in the French navy, fighting at Jersey (1779) and Gibraltar (1779–83).

Potemkin gave Nassau the credit for the victory in his report to Catherine; he praised Jones, 'but Nassau was the real hero and to him belongs the victory.'[4]

A further attempt to break the Russian blockade was made on 28 June. Hasan Pasha's flagship grounded, bringing the fleet to a halt. When the wind changed the following morning, the Russians launched an attack as the Ottoman ships dispersed in confusion. Another Ottoman ship was burnt for the loss of one Russian frigate. The Ottoman fleet withdrew under the guns of Ochakov, and then withdrew the larger vessels. However, nine of these then ran aground on the Kinburn Spit after being bombarded by Suvorov's cannon, and were destroyed the next day. Another Ottoman fleet arrived on 1 July, but withdrew on 9 July after failing to rescue the remaining smaller craft. The Ottomans lost over 3,000 dead, and a further 1,673 were taken prisoner.

The Ottomans engaged the Russian Sevastopol fleet on 14 July at the Battle of Fidonisi (known today as Snake Island). The Russian fleet was commanded by Marko Voynovich, with Fyodor Ushakov as his second-in-command. They had two ships of the line, ten frigates, and 24 small vessels. The Ottoman fleet, commanded by Hasan Pasha, consisted of 17 ships of the line, eight frigates, and 24 small vessels. Voynovich formed a line on the port tack, first heading northeast and then southeast as the wind veered. The Ottomans attacked from windward just after 3:00 pm. The Russian frigates *Berislav* (40) and *Stryela* (44) forced the leading Turks out of line, but were in danger of being cut off until Ushakov aboard *Sv. Pavel* (66) closed the gap. The Ottoman flagship was damaged in the subsequent fighting and had to withdraw from the line. The Ottoman fleet withdrew and returned to Ochakov, although they did manage to resupply and reinforce the garrison with 1,500 Janissaries.[5]

With the naval actions failing to break the siege, the Ottomans tried several land sorties. On 27 July, 5,000 Janissaries attacked the Russian trenches held by Cossacks, forcing them to retreat. However, Suvorov led a counterattack, driving them back to the fortress, although he was wounded, and some sources argue he was only saved by a diversion from Prince Repnin. Kutuzov also received his second head wound at the siege, a wound that would usually be fatal. However, the French surgeon Jean Massot performed miracles, although Kutuzov was blinded in one eye. The siege served as a training ground for many officers, and reads like a list of Russian generals from the Napoleonic Wars. Suvorov, as usual, favoured storming the fortress, responding to Potemkin's request for information with the

---

4. F. Golder, *John Paul Jones in Russia*, (Doubleday, 1927), p. 53.

5. The battle is depicted in the lavish Soviet-era film *Admiral Ushakov* (1953). Not entirely accurately, but it is worth the watching in full on YouTube with English sub-titles.

couplet 'I am sitting on a rock. And at Ochakov I look.' Potemkin was concerned about casualties, and he had Catherine's support in this cautious approach. He preferred to negotiate and starve fortresses into surrender. He was also happy to let the Austrians take the weight of the Ottoman attacks in the Balkans.

As winter began, both armies were suffering from the weather and disease, particularly dysentery. Temperatures fell to fifteen degrees centigrade, accompanied by snow and ice, and supplies of food ran short. Potemkin was criticised by foreign observers, who claimed exaggerated numbers of dead. However, the level of care was good for the period. As Montefiore argues, 'The army did suffer, many died, but Potemkin's medical care, money, food, clothes and humanitarianism, unparalleled in Russia, may explain the army's survival.'[6]

Russia was under military pressure from Sweden and by Prussian diplomatic actions in Poland. Catherine, therefore, urged Potemkin to capture Ochakov before moving into winter quarters. Potemkin gave in to the case for a storming, and on 6 December, infantry columns stormed the trenches and broke in through the Stamboul Gate. The Russian troops went mad, killing nearly 10,000 of the remaining garrison, including the commander, along with women and children. The Russians lost 956 dead and 1,829 wounded during the siege and assault, although some sources claim it was higher. The assault was commemorated in a Russian song, 'Turkish blood flowed like rivers, and the Pasha fell to his knees before Potemkin.' The booty was enormous, and Catherine was delighted: 'You've shut everybody's mouths, and this successful event gives you the chance to show generosity to those who criticise you blindly and stupidly.'

The Victory of Ochakov (Suchodolski)

---

6. S. Montefiore, *Prince of Princes: The Life of Potemkin*, (Phoenix Press, 2000), p. 411.

John Paul Jones

John Paul Jones was born near Kirkbean in south-west Scotland. He learned his trade in merchant ships, including the Atlantic slave trade, which he later described as 'abominable'. After two separate violent incidents with mutinous crew members, he fled to America and volunteered for the Continental Navy when the American War of Independence broke out in 1775.

He was appointed 1st lieutenant of the frigate USS Alfred, raiding in the West Indies. He next commanded the sloop Providence, transporting troops, escorting convoys, and capturing British merchant ships. After clashes with his superiors, he was transferred to the command of the sloop Ranger. He sailed to Europe and raided Whitehaven and Carrickfergus. In 1779, he was appointed to command the 42-gun Bonhomme Richard, donated by the French. Leading a small squadron, he attacked a convoy at the Battle of Flamborough Head, in which his ship was lost. He was decorated with the title 'Chevalier' by Louis XVI.

John Paul Jones

After the war, with no prospects, he entered Russian service in 1787, although some British officers, including Samuel Greig, refused to serve under him, considering him a pirate. Jones was to command a squadron in the Dneiper naval campaign with the rank of rear admiral. While he helped to defeat the Ottomans, he handled Russian politics less well than his ships, fell out with Potemkin, and was recalled to St. Petersburg. After being charged with rape in 1789, which he denied, he was sent abroad on a two-year leave by Catherine. He died in Paris in June 1792.

His entry in the Encyclopedia of American Biography concludes,

'In sum, Jones was a sailor of indomitable courage, of strong will, and of great ability in his chosen career. On the other side of the coin, it must be admitted that he was also a hypocrite, a brawler, a rake, and a professional and social climber. Although these elements of his character do not detract from his feats at sea, they do, perhaps, cast in doubt his eligibility for a prominent place in the ranks of America's immortals.'

Battles of Focşani and Rymnik 1789

Potemkin had moved to Moldavia to direct the next stage of the war. He was also able to direct Polish policy from there as well as liaise with the Austrians. Foreign policy was complicated by the French Revolution, with Catherine alarmed by the spread of the revolution's ideas. Negotiations with the Ottomans were going nowhere since they were temporarily boosted by Prussian support, until Frederick baulked at the prospect of a war with Russia.

In 1789, the Ottomans were being pushed back to new defensive lines in Moldavia and Wallachia. Sultan Abdul Hamid I died in April and was replaced by his nephew, Selim III. Grand Vizier Koca Yusuf Pasha faced an Austrian army of 18,000 men coming from Transylvania, led by Prince Josias of Coburg, and a Russian division of 7,000 men commanded by Suvorov, coming from Jassy. Yusuf Pasha decided to attack the Austrians before the allies could link up. He ordered Osman Pasha to lead an army of 30,000 men north to Focşani (modern Romania), a trade centre on the Wallachian/Moldavian border. However, Suvorov marched his division 40 miles in 28 hours to reach Coburg and the Austrian position on the Siret River, north of the town.

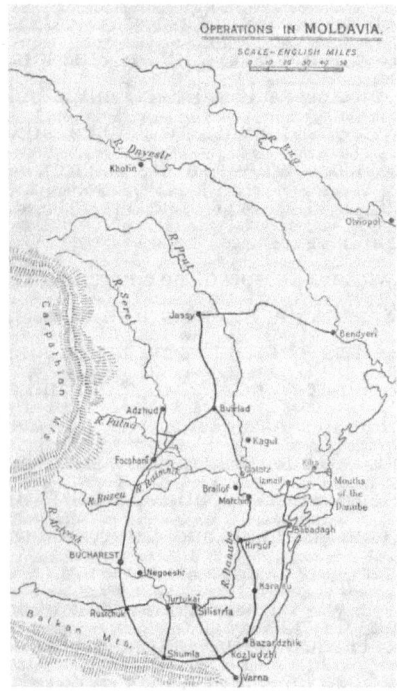
Operations in Moldovia

The Austrians had adopted the Russian tactics of fighting the Ottomans in squares, after their poor performance in the Austro-Ottoman War (1737–39). They advanced with the Russians in two columns on 31 July, driving the Ottoman outposts back to their main position at Focşani, then crossed the river and deployed in two lines of squares with cavalry and artillery in between. The battle started at 9:00 am on 1 August with an artillery bombardment of the Ottoman entrenchments. The Ottomans left their trenches to attack the allies in front and on both flanks, but were driven back. Suvorov employed the Russian cavalry to attack the Ottoman right flank. While they were repulsed, the following infantry attack, using marshy ground to conceal their movements, successfully pushed the Ottomans back into their trenches. The Austrians achieved a similar success on the Ottoman left, and by 4:00 pm the Ottoman army had fled. The Ottomans lost 1,500 dead and 2,500 wounded. Allied casualties totalled 800.

The Russians and Austrians were too exhausted to pursue, allowing the Ottomans to regroup further south at Braila. Suvorov returned to his base at Buirlad.

The loss of Moldavia led to Yusuf Pasha being replaced as grand vizier by Cenaze Hasan Pasha. He reinforced the main field army to a strength of around 100,000 men, including 40,000 Janissaries, 40,000 cavalry, and 20,000 other infantry, supported by 85 guns. He started the new offensive with a night march from Braila to attack Coburg's 18,000-strong Austrian army on the Râmnicul Sărat River in Wallachia, south of Focşani. Coburg managed to fight off the initial attack from the Ottoman vanguard on 19 September and called on Suvorov's 7,000-strong division for support. He replied, 'Coming, Suvorov' and quickly marched to their aid, covering about 97 kilometres in two and a half days, arriving on 21 September. The Ottomans had camped in the river basin of the Rymna (Râmna) and Rymnik Rivers, fortifying three camps six kilometres apart. Despite being outnumbered four to one, Suvorov proposed attacking and defeating the larger Ottoman army in piecemeal fashion.

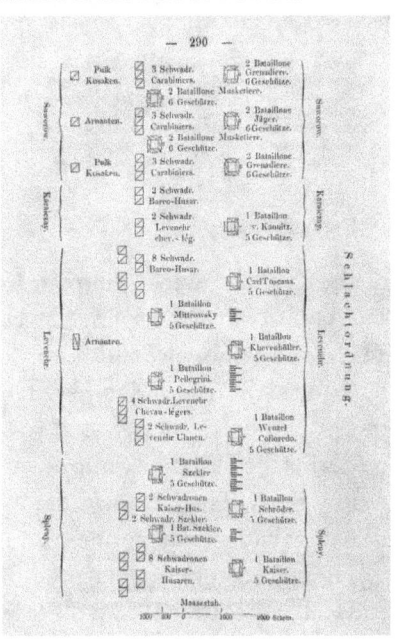

Order of Battle, Focşani 1789 (August von Witzleben)

On the evening of 21 September, Russian engineers discovered a crossing point on the Rymna, and Suvorov led his column across the river, forming into six squares, three in each line. They advanced six kilometres south towards the Ottoman camp at Tyrgo Kukuli. After an artillery exchange, some 12,000 Ottoman troops surged out of a gully to attack the Russian left flank. One square was breached in several places, but after reserves and fire support were deployed from the neighbouring square, the Ottomans retreated, pursued by Russian and Austrian cavalry. Suvorov moved his division to the left to support Coburg, who had also crossed the river but was under attack from around 40,000 Ottoman troops. The grand vizier, from his position on a ridge, could see a gap between the Russian and Austrian forces and attempted to exploit it. Suvorov's column was attacked near the village of Bogza (Vrancea) by around 6,000 Ottoman troops, and the assault was only driven off by repeated cavalry counterattacks.

Battle of Rymnik

The Austrians were facing difficulties, with their left wing surrounded, when Suvorov arrived. He aligned his forces on the Austrian right, and a six-kilometre allied line advanced towards the Ottoman entrenchments. Russian carabinier cavalry charged through the gaps in the Russian squares and captured the earthworks, forcing the remaining Ottoman troops to retreat to their camp on the Rymnik River and into the Kryngior Melor wood. A further Ottoman attack was repulsed as the allied line slowly advanced. The Ottoman troops started to drift away from the battle, and having attempted to rally them, the grand vizier also abandoned the field and retreated back to Braila. By nightfall, the allies had secured the ground up to the Rymnik River. A limited pursuit began the following day, capturing the Ottoman camp as well as more retreating troops as they tried to cross nearby rivers. The Ottoman dead were around 15,000, along with the loss of 67 field guns and a vast amount of equipment.

The twin victories at Focşani and Rymnik secured Suvorov's military reputation, and Catherine awarded him the title 'Count of Rymnik' (Rymniksky). His letter of thanks was typically gushing: 'I am now like a newly enrolled recruit, ready to give up my life for you. When by divine decree it comes to me to take leave of life and my Motherland, I shall have nothing but God and great Catherine! May the lustre of this most famous age of your monarchy extend to the last of time! May your might establish blessings in Europe and the whole world!'[7]

Monument to Suvorov looking over the Rymnik battlefield (Author)

The Austrians had also learned how to fight the Ottomans effectively, and they occupied Wallachia until the end of the war. The Ottoman Grand Vizier Cenaze Hasan Pasha was dismissed on 2 December and replaced by Cezayirli Gazi Hasan Pasha. Potemkin used these victories to move down the Dniester River, capturing the fortresses of Akkerman and Bender through negotiated surrenders. It was a very Potemkin outcome. The sultan was less impressed by the surrender of a 20,000-man garrison and had the commander executed.

---

7. 9 November 1789, quoted in B. Blease, *Suvorof*, (Constable, 1920), p. 108.

Potemkin posted Kutuzov to Akkerman for a role that gets little attention in wars of this period, intelligence operations. Kutuzov was given access to special funds to recruit agents in enemy territory. He also formed small squads of Cossacks that infiltrated behind enemy lines and returned with information about Ottoman troop concentrations. He may have personally taken part in some of these missions, and in July reported that he had personally observed the Ottoman fleet arriving in the Dniester estuary.[8]

Siege of Izmail, December 1790

The Russians continued the advance, capturing the fortresses of Kilia, Tulcea, and Isaktcha in the Danube Delta. They then targeted the major Ottoman fortress and port at Izmail (in modern Ukraine on the north bank of the Danube).

Meanwhile, the Austrians agreed to attack the Ottoman fortresses at Orşova and Giurgiu on the Danube, thereby distracting the Ottomans with a river crossing. Orşova fell on 7 April, and Coburg advanced his force of 15,000 men (nine infantry battalions, 16 squadrons of cavalry) slowly towards Giurgiu. The Ottoman garrison commanded by Çavuşzade Abdullah Pasha had only 4,000 men. However, the fortress had been modernised, and the siege guns had little effect. On 10 June, the Ottomans surprised the forward siege battery with a sortie of only 400 men. They followed this up with a more substantial attack, which routed five infantry battalions and killed the Austrian artillery commander. Coburg was on the river when this happened, surveying the banks, and when he returned, he had little option but to abandon the siege. General Clerfayt recovered the Austrian position somewhat by a victory over the Turks at Calafat (opposite Vidin on the Danube) in June. However, this ended Austrian operations.

The attack on Izmail was helped by the Russian naval victory at the Battle of Tendra on 8–9 September 1790. The Russian fleet of ten ships of the line, six frigates, and small craft sailed from Sevastopol on 5 September, commanded by Ushakov. They encountered the Ottoman fleet of 14 ships of the line, eight frigates, and 23 small crafts at anchor near Tendra Spit in the Black Sea off the Ukrainian coast.

---

8. A. Mikaberidze, *Kutuzov: A Life in War and Peace*, (Oxford, 2022), p. 65.

Battle of Tendra 8–9 September 1790 (By Afanasy de Paldo)

The Russian fleet focused on the tail end of the Ottoman fleet, forcing them to turn north and form a parallel line to the Russians, with both fleets heading northeast. The subsequent firefight lasted over three hours before the Ottomans disengaged, taking advantage of their superior speed to escape. Two damaged ships of the line were captured the next day. The victory at Tendra gave the Russians naval control of the Black Sea, enabling them to conduct operations against Ottoman positions on the coast. The weakest part of the Izmail defences was on the river, which the Ottoman fleet could no longer defend.

Izmail had been captured by Nikolai Repnin in 1770, but the Ottomans had rebuilt the fortress after the war with advice from German and French engineers. The sultan claimed it was impregnable, a boast that was always unwise. While foreign observers described its formidable fortifications, it had weaknesses. Some of the works had not been completed, and the riverside was defended by a simple parapet, making it vulnerable to assault from the other side of the river. It was garrisoned by a claimed 35,000 troops and 265 guns, commanded by Aydoslu Mehmed Pasha. However, this is probably later propaganda as intelligence reports indicated a garrison of around 15,000, including 10,000 Janissaries, all in poor condition with high desertion rates. The Russians had amassed 16,000 regulars and 15,000 irregulars for the siege. Potemkin assigned Lieutenant-General Ivan Gudovich to the siege, but little progress was made. He therefore brought Suvorov, who was sealing off Braila, down the Danube to take command, just as the Russian commanders had started to withdraw. Potemkin wrote to Suvorov, 'My hope is in God and your bravery. According to my orders to you, your presence on the spot will unite all parties. There are many generals there of equal rank, everywhere the cause of a sort of nest of indecision. Survey and arrange everything. Pray God and set to work. There are weak spots, if only you go together.'

Suvorov arrived on 13 December and organised his troops around the fortress with his flanks resting on the river. The Deribas Flotilla controlled the river itself along with a detachment of artillery and infantry on Çatal Island. Siege batteries were established (although only equipped with field guns) to deceive the Ottoman garrison into thinking this would be a formal siege, while troops were trained in escalade techniques, out of sight. The Russians bombarded the town on 21 September from the river and land. The Ottoman response achieved some success, blowing up the frigate *Konstantin,* and daily cavalry sorties further exacerbated Russian difficulties. The Ottoman guns were largely silenced by 3:00 am, although there was no breach in the walls, as the Russian guns were not heavy enough.

Suvorov convened a council of war, less for consultation and more for inspiration, saying, 'Twice have the Russians approached Izmail, and twice they have retreated. Now, the third time, all we can do is either take the city or die trying.' The Russian assault started at dawn on 22 December. The right wing columns (7,500 men), were commanded by Pavel Potemkin, and the left wing (12,000 men), commanded by Alexander Samoilov. Kutuzov led five battalions (three Jager and two grenadier) and 1,000 dismounted Cossacks to seize the rampart at the Kilya Gate, close to the river on the Russian far left. The naval flotilla commanded by Iosif Deribas attacked from the riverside, with one column assaulting the New Fortress, the middle column aiming for the centre of the coastal front, and the left column the Old Fortress. The cavalry (2,500 men) was held in reserve. Each column had an echelon with fascines to help cross the moat, followed by another with scaling ladders, leaving the third echelon to make the assault and a fourth to give covering fire.

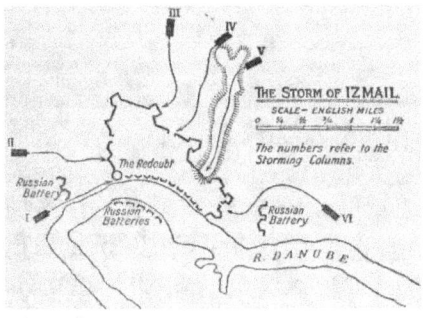

The initial assaults faltered under fierce defensive fire from the Ottoman garrison, who had been warned of the assault by deserters. The moat in places was deeper than expected, and the ladders were too short. On the right flank, one column had lost its way and attacked one of the strongest bastions. The most successful assault was on the less well-defended riverside wall. By 8:00 am, Russian troops had established a foothold on the ramparts and three of the city's gates were opened, allowing the cavalry reserve to enter. The Ottoman troops fought for every street, and counter-attacks were sent out from the Old Fortress. However, by 4:00 pm, the city and fortress had fallen. Among the dead in the last stand were the Tatar prince, Kaplan Giray, and his five sons.

Suvorov allowed three days of slaughter and plunder of what was a wealthy town, the loot totalling at least one million roubles—a vast sum equivalent to the annual pay of 100,000 Russian soldiers. Most of the garrison and civilians (including Christians, contrary to Suvorov's orders) were killed. It took six days to clear the 26,000 (some sources say 40,000) dead, mainly into the river. Russian casualties were officially 1,815 dead and 2,445 wounded, although they were probably much higher. Several commanders reported that two-thirds of their officers were casualties. As Duffy describes it, 'One of the bloodiest days of the century.'[9]

Kutuzov was appointed the commandant of the fortress as a reward for his courage in the storming, along with a medal and nomination for a promotion to lieutenant general. The unofficial Russian national anthem in the late eighteenth and early nineteenth centuries, *Grom pobedy, razdavaysya!* ('Let the thunder of victory sound!') was dedicated to the victory. It is still commemorated as a Day of Military Honour in Russia. The victory and the slaughter were widely commented on across Europe. The siege is dramatised in Byron's verse-novel *Don Juan* (1823).[10]

All was prepared—the fire, the sword, the men
To wield them in their terrible array—
The army, like a lion from his den,
Marched forth with nerve and sinews bent to slay—
A human Hydra, issuing from its fen
To breathe destruction on its winding way,
Whose heads were heroes, which cut off in vain
Immediately in others grew again.

The Battle of Măcin and Peace

After Izmail, both armies went into winter quarters. The Russians were concerned that Prussia might declare war, and the British issued an ultimatum. However, there was parliamentary and military resistance to sending a fleet, including by Nelson, and the ultimatum was withdrawn in April. The Polish revolutionaries were still a challenge on the same front, and Potemkin was prepared to buy the Prussians off, but Catherine was not. This strained their relationship, but it was not a complete break, as some argue. Sultan Selim III also recognised that his army and navy were in no position to continue the conflict.

---

9. C. Duffy, *Russia's Military Way to the West*, (Routledge, 1981), p. 188.

10. Lord Byron, *Don Juan* (Canto VII & VIII, Standard EBooks, 2024).

On the Danube front, Nikolai Repnin was placed in command as Potemkin returned to St. Petersburg. In April, Kutuzov sallied out of Izmail. With 3,000 infantry and 1,300 Cossacks, he dispersed the Ottoman forces, covering his troops, and pushed them back to the Ottoman base at Babadag. He then linked up with Golitsyn, defeating an Ottoman force led by Deli Pasha at Luncavița. In pursuing the fleeing Ottoman troops, they reached and captured the town of Măcin. This relatively easy victory encouraged a bolder advance to the fortress at Brăila, storming the forts on the east bank of the Danube. Here they were joined by de Ribas's flotilla, which helped to transport troops to an island closer to the fortress, but the garrison's guns were too strong for the Russian ships. While they could bombard the town, there was no prospect of the Ottomans surrendering a key base, and the Russians returned to Izmail.

In early June, reports of growing Ottoman strength persuaded Repnin to order Kutuzov to make another attack on Babadag, this time with 12,000 men. Kutuzov faced around 15,000 Ottomans outside Babadag, and beat off successive attacks by forming squares. The Ottomans abandoned the town and its supplies. Kutuzov had won his first battle in independent command.

The Ottoman army had concentrated at Măcin, around 65,000 strong, commanded by Seraskir Mustafa, with the new Grand Vizier Koca Yusef Pasha due to arrive from Hîrșova. This was his second term in the role after the defeat at Foscani. Repnin marched his army towards the town and launched an attack in three columns. Prince Golitsyn attacked the Ottoman left flank, Prince Volkonsky's troops took the Turkish camp in the centre, and Kutuzov, on the Turkish right, was to deliver the decisive blow. The Russians advanced in their now-standard chequerboard squares, with cavalry in between. The Ottoman cavalry charged the squares for several hours, pinning the two main Russian columns.

The view from the site of the Măcin citadel today, with the heights in the background. (Author)

Kutuzov's troops worked their way up the high ground on the Ottoman right, under heavy fire and sustained attacks by infantry and cavalry. Repnin was considering a withdrawal when a Russian artillery detachment repulsed an Ottoman flank attack from Braila. They sank elements of the landing force while crossing the river, and reserves arrived to push the Ottomans back. Volkonsky sent two grenadier regiments to plug the growing gap between his column and Kutuzov's. The confusion created by this attack enabled Kutuzov to reach the heights and reorganise his force into five squares supported by cavalry. They fought off fresh Ottoman attacks and advanced down the hill towards the town. With his flank turned, Mustafa ordered a retreat before the grand vizier could arrive with 20,000 reinforcements.

This was the final land battle of the war, with Ottoman casualties of around 4,000, and the Russians reported 431, although it was likely to have been higher. Repnin gave much of the credit to Kutuzov. Writing to Catherine, he praised his tactical decisions, moving in columns, forming squares, and coordinating with his cavalry and artillery. 'They testify to his ability to read the terrain and use it to his advantage, assess the battle situation, and react swiftly to changes.'[11] Kutuzov's reputation was made.

There was one final naval clash at Cape Kaliakra on 11 August 1791. Kaliakra is a cape in the Southern Dobruja region of the modern Bulgarian Black Sea Coast. Ushakov had taken the Russian fleet of 15 ships of the line and two frigates from Sevastopol on 8 August. He encountered the Ottoman fleet, commanded by Hussein Pasha, consisting of 18 ships of the line and 17 frigates, at anchor just south of Cape Kaliakra, protected by a fort and coastal batteries. Ushakov attacked in three columns from the northeast, thereby separating the Ottomans from the cape. The Ottoman fleet weighed anchor and sailed east, with the Russians following in a parallel east-south-east course. The fighting began at 4:45 pm as the Ottoman fleet manoeuvred south. Darkness put an end to the fighting at 8:30 pm, and the Ottoman fleet broke off, heading back to Constantinople. Neither side lost a ship, although several were damaged.

Prince Repnin agreed to an eight-month truce on 31 July 1791, and negotiations began on a peace treaty. Potemkin believed that Repnin, who was unaware that the Prussian and British threat had been neutralised, had conceded too much, and that such a long truce would give the Ottomans time to recover. Repnin was also unaware of Ushakov's victory at Kaliakra. The Treaty of Jassy (Iași) was signed on 9 January 1792 by Grand Vizier Koca Yusuf Pasha and Prince Bezborodko. Potemkin had fallen ill in September while in the fever-ridden city of Jassy, probably with bronchial pneumonia, while overseeing the peace talks. Potemkin was travelling to Nikolayev on 16 October (aged fifty-two) when he died in the open steppe, sixty kilometres from Iași, an appropriate place for the man who had been the driving force of Russian colonisation of the steppe. Catherine was distraught at the news, exclaiming, 'How can I replace Potemkin?' Grand Duke Paul and many of the old nobility quietly celebrated. After Catherine died in 1796, Paul ordered the destruction of Potemkin's grave and many of his reforms. However, the grave survived in St. Catherine's Cathedral in Kherson, although the remains may have been removed during the modern conflict.

---

11. A. Mikaberidze, *Kutuzov: A Life in War and Peace*, (Oxford, 2022), p. 92.

The Treaty of Jassy confirmed the Russian annexation of Crimea. Yedisan (the territory between the Dniester and Bug rivers) was transferred to Russia, establishing the Dniester as the Russo-Ottoman border in Europe, while leaving the Asiatic frontier (the Kuban River) unchanged. The Ottomans also acknowledged Georgia (the Kingdom of Kartli-Kakheti) as a Russian protectorate.

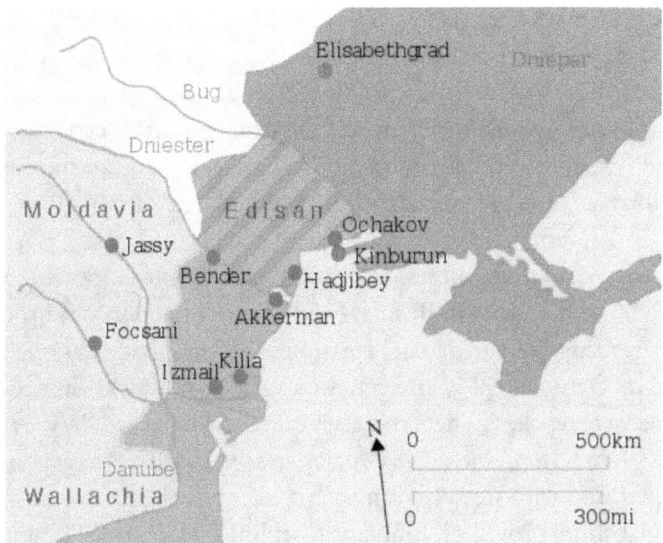

Border changes agreed in the Treaty of Jassy 1792 (Cplakidas-derivative work: Jarry125)

Austro-Ottoman War

The Austrians reached a separate peace in the Treaty of Sistova on 4 August 1791. They were most directly threatened by Prussian intervention in the conflict, and their gains were modest: a strip of Croatian land near the Bosnian-Croatian border. We have covered the actions of the Austrian army in the campaigns examined in this study, but there was a broader series of campaigns that impacted the ability of both the Austrians and the Ottomans to conduct operations. Austria (under Emperor Joseph II) joined the war against the Ottomans primarily to expand its territory in the Balkans and to recover from its setbacks in the Austro-Ottoman War of 1737–1739.

The Austrians had mobilised a large army of approximately 245,000 men in six corps across the frontier with the Ottomans, although significant forces had to be retained in the north to face Prussia. They could not begin military operations until

May 1789. The army also had to face an epidemic. The plague took the largest death toll in the Slovak corps, where, in February, 1,090 soldiers of infantry and 79 cavalry lost their lives. By the end of May, 5,619 people stayed in Croatian quarantine areas, and a fifth of the Croatian army was incapable of fighting.

The main Austrian effort would be in Bosnia and on the Danube between Belgrade, Orşova, and Vidin, while the Russians focused on Moldavia. The siege of Belgrade in 1788 progressed slowly, and was abandoned when the Ottomans broke into the Banat and threatened the rear of the Austrian armies. Worse was to come during the 'Battle' of Karánsebes (Caransebeş) on 21–22 September when portions of the Austrian army, which were scouting, fired on one another by mistake, causing self-inflicted casualties, and allowing the Ottomans to capture the city. This has been described as 'history's worst friendly fire incident', although the details are contested.[12]

The Austrians had more success in Croatia and Slavonia, capturing Šabac (Schabatz) in Serbia and Dubica in Bosnia. Field Marshal Laudon was brought out of retirement, capturing Novi Grad in September 1788. Belgrade was finally captured by Laudon in October 1789, and renewed Ottoman attacks on the Banat and Transylvania were repelled. These successes came at a high cost. Between June 1788 and May 1789 alone, there were 172,000 sick and wounded on the army lists, 33,000 of whom died, and with steadily-rising recruitment demands, unrest was growing in various Habsburg provinces. Emperor Joseph II's death in 1790, along with the Prussian threat and internal conflict, led Austria to the peace table.

---

12. C. Martin, *Can it be true? Did Austria really attack itself?* (History is Now, 5 March 2017).

Chapter Thirteen

Conclusion

The Treaty of Kuchuk Kainardji has been described as 'one of the most fateful documents of Ottoman history,' even allowing for the contested interpretation of the treaty.[1] The Russian victory came at enormous cost, with casualties of over 500,000 on both sides. It also set the scene for the second conflict, which resulted in a further 200,000 killed on both sides. The Treaty of Iași confirmed and expanded Russia's territorial gains across the Pontic steppe and secured its access to the Black Sea. This enabled the rapid colonisation of the region.

The wars were a disaster for the Balkans. Urban and rural areas were devastated, populations scattered, and those remaining were impoverished by taxes and war requisitions. Not that this disturbed Catherine's grand vision. As she wrote to Voltaire, 'We are at war, it is true: but Russia has long been used to that occupation, and emerges from each war in a more flourishing state than before.'

The Russian victory in both wars can be credited to its infantry regiments, including line, grenadiers, and jägers. Irregular troops, particularly the Cossacks, were brought into the army system and performed key roles on the borders. Russia also benefited from outstanding leadership, with innovative commanders such as Rumyantsev, Potemkin, and Suvorov. It was the army that carried state power into the Pontic steppe, allowing the administrators to develop the newly conquered lands economically, often using ex-soldiers as settlers and local militias. The civil and military powers were, at least in the early stages, intertwined. In contrast, the Ottomans never developed the same border defences. The armed forces were separate from the peasantry, and their operations often drove the latter from the land.

The Russian victory was aided by the Ottoman army's deterioration, caused by its failure to reform and the prolonged period of peace preceding the 1768 war.

---

1. Shaw, S., *History of the Ottoman Empire and Modern Turkey, Volume 1*, (Cambridge, 1976), p. 250.

As Aksan concludes, 'Uncoordinated command, and the constant insubordination of the troops, who preferred pillage and desertion to sustained attack, paralysed the Ottoman war effort.'[2] All too often, at the first enemy volley, the raw recruits fled. They were also undermined by a breakdown of the Ottoman supply system, exacerbated by the weather. The Ottoman strengths included the ability to dig trenches at a speed that amazed the Russian commanders. They also had the edge in fortress defence, in which outstanding commanders could inspire their troops to resist larger and better-equipped Russian besiegers, when they were adequately supplied.

While modern scholarship largely rejects the traditional theory of Ottoman decline over several centuries, it is the case that the Empire failed to progress and develop compared to its adversaries in the eighteenth century. They lacked the cohesiveness of the major European powers and faced internal obstacles to industrialisation and centralisation. By the end of our period, the Ottoman government had only limited control over large swathes of the nominal empire, with semi-autonomous rulers becoming the real power centres. Radical attempts at reform faced opposition from conservative interests, although minor changes were achieved by striking a balance among various traditional interests. They also faced external pressures on almost every front that even a centralised European power would have struggled to manage. The last sultans of our period, Abdul Hamid I and Selim III, introduced military reforms, which, although not sustained, set the stage for substantive reforms in the nineteenth century.

War, famine, and plague also played significant roles in undermining the Ottoman economy and, consequently, its ability to wage war. This is reflected in the demographics of the Empire during this period, exacerbated by waves of migration. Muslims were driven from Hungary, Tatars from Russia, and Christian Serbs and Bosnians moved north into the Habsburg lands, a process accelerated during the war against Austria. The population of the Balkans, once the economic powerhouse of the Empire, fell from eight million in the late sixteenth century to three million by the mid-eighteenth century. This is reflected in the declining population of both cities and the countryside, even allowing for the drift to urban areas as banditry increased in the countryside. Even the population of Constantinople may have halved during the same period. In Greece, the revolts and the subsequent atrocities committed by Albanian soldiers caused a further exodus. The medieval-style agrarian economy had already struggled to provide the tax base and surpluses needed by a modern state, even before these other factors. Western contemporaries were developing economies based on commerce and banking, which generated revenues that the Ottomans could not match.

---

2. V. Aksan, *Ottoman Wars 1700–1870*, (Pearson, 2007), p. 153.

Despite all of these challenges, the Ottoman Empire did not collapse during the 1787 war and the Balkans were not partitioned like Poland. The Ottomans defeated Austrian armies and held off the Russians for long enough to secure a peace. The big losers were the Pontic steppe nomads, whose way of life was replaced by colonisation and agriculture. The old open frontier zone had disappeared after these wars. Colonial attitudes were evident in the Caucasus, with a Russian general in 1768 refusing to negotiate with Kabardinian nobles because 'it was below his dignity to speak to such people.' He was reflecting a colonial discourse, not unique to Russia, which regarded the natives as wild animals to be tamed. Catherine's instructions stated, first, 'restrain the local unbridled peoples from raids and predations,' and later, 'cajole the savage peoples to be under our rule.'[3] This also reflected a mission to bring the inseparable (in Russian eyes) concepts of civilisation and Christianity to indigenous peoples.

At significant human and financial cost, the Russians made their colonial advances self-funding. As historian William McNeill explains, 'The fiscally self-sustaining character of the process does much to explain its success. A hard-working, submissive peasantry, tax collectors under enough discipline to make them channel resources as directed by central authorities, and central authorities interested in using their power to forward settlement, were all required for the system to work.'[4] Technology, such as steel plough shares, played a role, but it was the social organisation, coupled with better distribution through roads and ports, that made the real difference. As Gabor Agostan argues, 'In the patrimonial Ottoman Empire of the 16th century, the sultan and his central government had more control over their empire's resources and the means of organized violence than their Muscovite counterparts...by the 18th century, Istanbul lost its edge over St. Petersburg.'[5]

These wars confirmed that the Ottoman Empire was now firmly on the defensive, facing less divided and less distracted opponents than in the previous century. More directly, the treaties marked a significant shift in the power balance on the Pontic steppe and the Black Sea, which had previously been under Ottoman control. Catherine's grand vision of a new Byzantine Empire was never achieved, but the Balkans would remain a battleground into the next century.

---

3. M. Khodarkovsky, *Russia's Steppe Frontier*, (Indiana Press, 2004), p. 187.

4. W. McNeill, *Europe's Steppe Frontier, 1500–1800*, (Chicago, 1964), p. 185.

5. G. Agostan, *Military Transformation in the Ottoman Empire and Russia, 1500–1800*, (Kritika: Explorations in Russia and Eurasian History, 12:2, Spring 2011), p. 282.

Chapter Fourteen

Annex: Wargaming the Conflict

Introduction

Wargamers use model soldiers to simulate battles, real or fictional. The game evolved from chess and the military war games used by the Prussian general staff in the nineteenth century. The modern hobby began in the 1950s, and despite the rise of computer and board games, it remains a thriving hobby today, with monthly magazines and hundreds of clubs worldwide. The modern military also uses wargames to simulate strategic and tactical decisions as a learning tool and to test operational responses.

Unlike chess, there are hundreds of different rule sets, each covering a specific historical period; however, around fifty are played in significant numbers. They usually start with a points system for each army to create a balanced game, as well as rules for setting out the battlefield terrain. Once the troops are on the table, the rules set out how fast each unit can move, followed by rules for shooting and then hand-to-hand combat. Records are kept for casualties, or figures are removed from the table. Finally, rules determine the morale of each unit and the army as a whole. Dice or cards of various types are used to determine the chance element.

The figures are generally made of metal or plastic and are hand-painted. In a historical game, this involves researching the army's uniforms, organisation, and tactics. The models come in various sizes, from 2mm to 54mm high, and are made by figure manufacturers worldwide, or increasingly produced at home using 3D printers. Most wargamers have many different armies that they collect on a project basis. For a detailed introduction to this fascinating hobby, the reader can do no better than consulting *The Wargaming Compendium* by Henry Hyde (Pen & Sword, 2013).

Russian square being attacked by Tatars

For the wargamer, the Russo-Ottoman Wars offer a wide range of options. There were major battles in the Balkans, a war of outposts for skirmish games, and naval actions. There were a variety of troop types, from Russian regulars and Janissaries to irregular troops including Tatars and Cossacks. The revolts in Greece and the Levant bring another group of colourful troop types to the tabletop.

Wargame Rules

Many different rule sets can be used for this period, which can be daunting, so we will focus on the most widely played systems. All rules are a balance between simulation and playability, with modern practice leaning more towards the latter. This approach abstracts many of the factors that comprise warfare to expedite play. Modern rules are generally designed to be played in an evening over two to three hours, on a table no bigger than six or eight feet wide. Wargamers refer to the period covered by the Russo-Ottoman Wars as the horse and musket, or the tricorne, era. It reflects the introduction of the socket bayonet, which allowed infantry to deliver effective firepower in linear formations (or squares) and still defend themselves against cavalry, much like pikes and spears did in earlier conflicts. As we have seen, it was Russian infantry firepower, supported by lighter artillery, that won most battles. That doesn't mean that cavalry was not effective, but they increasingly relied on the charge to make contact quickly. By the late eighteenth century, even European armies had adopted light and irregular troops to adapt to the terrain and the vast distances involved on the Pontic Steppe. Wargame rules for the Napoleonic period can often be adapted for this period, but the French Revolutionary Wars introduced new tactics, including columns, that were not typically deployed in the eighteenth century.

Many of the battles in these wars were huge. Ottoman armies could field 50–80,000 men over a battlefield several miles wide. With large amounts of cavalry, they could also cover significant distances. This requires either scaling the battle down to a manageable size by making each unit represent a larger number of troops or fighting just one aspect of the battle. Alternatively, use a smaller scale model figure (6mm, 10mm, or 15mm), and reduce the move and firing distances accordingly. Probably the most popular set of rules for this period is *Black Powder* (Warlord Games), written by Rick Priestley and Jervis Johnson. A typical game involves three brigades (or you can scale up to divisions), with three to five units in each brigade, consisting of 18–24 figures. The system is highly flexible, and its basic mechanisms are easy to learn. These rules are our go-to set for larger battles, although we have also been playtesting *Lust for Glory* by Simon Miller. These are an adaptation of his popular *To the Strongest* rules for the ancient and medieval periods, utilising a grid system that can speed up play. They replace dice with playing cards to introduce the chance factor. Another popular approach for larger games is *Maurice* by Sam Mustafa, which comes with a pack of action cards which can be played at different stages of the game.

Outside the major battles, the Russian and Ottoman forces engaged in a war of outposts, or smaller actions. For this, we need skirmish rules that can involve anything for twenty to eighty figures on each side. This is a good way to get into the hobby, as games can be set up and played quickly, and you don't need to paint large numbers of models. *Sharp Practice* by Richard Clark (Too Fat Lardies) is a popular ruleset for large skirmishes, focusing on building characters and a narrative for your games. As the author puts it, 'It is better to die bravely than a coward, but sometimes dying humorously can be better still.' These rules emphasise command and control rather than the minutiae of weaponry. Osprey Wargames publishes Dan Mersey's *Rebels and Patriots*, which, although designed for North America, works very well for our purposes. The mix of regular and irregular forces is similar to that in the Russo-Ottoman wars, and the game mechanics are straightforward, allowing new players to grasp the basics in a couple of moves. If you have only collected a handful of figures, then *Fistful of Lead* (Wiley Games) is an excellent introductory skirmish game typically played with six to eight figures on each side. These fast and furious, card-activated rules are a fantastic way to engage your kids in the hobby.

As the narrative of the campaigns in this book highlights, sieges were an essential part of eighteenth-century warfare. The French engineer Vauban designed his forts with multiple star-shaped bastions, with a lower profile than the classic medieval castle. All nations extensively copied this style of fortification, and the Ottomans brought in French engineers to upgrade their medieval fortresses. A formal siege, such as the one at Ochakov, could take many months while the besiegers advanced closer to the walls by digging zig-zag trenches and temporary gun positions to create a breach in the walls. These would then be stormed.

Fire and Stone (Capstone Games)

This type of warfare is challenging to replicate on the tabletop due to the scale and time involved. Options include board games like the excellent *Fire and Stone: Siege of Vienna 1683* (Capstone Games), or playing a section of the siege, including one of the frequent sorties that the defending forces used to disrupt the besiegers' progress.

Naval actions played a crucial role in these wars, both in the Mediterranean and the Black Sea. These included fleet actions and smaller operations linked to the land campaigns. Naval wargaming can be complex, with rules covering the minutiae of manoeuvring a sailing ship across the table. Wargamers on land do not have to worry about wind, currents, or rocks, as troops generally move as ordered. Gabrio Tolentino has successfully abstracted these complications in *Black Seas* (Warlord Games). The supplement to these rules, *Hold Fast!*, covers the more minor battles involving frigates, brigs, sloops, and galleys. They also include lists for the Russians and Ottomans, which are often overlooked in fleet battle rules. There are more detailed rules, but these are a good starting point.

Ottoman galleys (Warlord games)

Most rules for this period are designed for the European battlefields of the Seven Years' War, or colonial conflicts in India and North America. They often struggle with troop types like Janissaries, which don't fit into the European model. You may have to tweak your favourite rules system to accommodate them.

A modern set of wargame rules can cost between £20 and £30, with full colour printing, and the add-ons like action cards or special dice add to the cost. A cost-effective option is the Osprey Wargames series that typically costs less than £12. *Honours of War* is a ruleset that would work for our period. Alternatively, the *Wargames Vault* (www.wargamevault.com) has many sets of rules to get you started, with PDF downloads under £10.

While we have focused on tabletop games, we should not forget wargame campaigns. These can be as complex as you want or simply a mechanism for linking your tabletop battles. Many of the rules above have simple campaign systems. However, if you're going to tackle this subject in detail, then Henry Hyde's *Wargaming Campaigns* (Pen & Sword, 2022) shows you how. Board games are another way of tackling campaigns, although we are not aware of any that specifically cover these wars.

Wargame Figures

If you have got this far, you will be looking for some wargame figures to manoeuvre around the tabletop. If money is no object, then there are secondhand figures to be purchased on eBay, and plenty of professional figure painters will turn your metal or plastic figures into the finished product. However, for most wargamers, this involves purchasing and painting the figures. Uniform colours are generally available on the internet or in the books listed in the bibliography. There are numerous how-to guides on painting on YouTube and elsewhere that guide beginners through the basics. With modern paints and washes, very presentable results can be achieved without needing an art degree. It is also a very therapeutic aspect of the hobby, the perfect way to wind down after a busy day. The best advice is to start with a small number of figures and build your collection as time and budget allow.

For those of a certain age, the early years of the hobby involved getting catalogues from a few manufacturers or using the ubiquitous boxes of 1/72nd figures in the Airfix range. Today, the wargamer has a vast array of ranges to choose from in every figure scale, covering just about every troop type and ships as well.

The first decision is the figure scale. If you want to fight the larger battles in our region, the smaller scales are the best choice. There are 6mm ranges from Baccus and Adler. Do not worry about painting too much detail at this scale; you will be looking at the models from a couple of feet away, not through a magnifying glass. Slightly larger with more detail are the 10mm ranges from Pendraken. For the divisional games, 15mm is a good option. Essex and Old Glory have comprehensive ranges. As do Eureka, although they are slightly larger at 18mm. For the smaller battles and skirmish games, 28mm figures are ideal. There are ranges by Front Rank, Foundry, and Claymore Castings, although not so extensive as to include Russian Jagers. For Ottomans and Cossacks, it is worth examining the Renaissance period ranges, as these figures will typically apply to these wars. Plastic figures are popular and cheaper, but are rare in this period. There are Prussian and Austrian figures, as well as American War of Independence ranges, that could work for the Russians with some conversion work. For ships, Warlord makes all you will need in their *Black Seas* range. For finer-detail models, Langton Miniatures does a comprehensive range in 1:1,200 scale, although these require some modelling skills.

Russians in Potemkin uniforms (North Star)

You will also need a mat for your table. A simple light green or sandy cloth will suffice, and blue is suitable for naval battles, although there are some better options available from Deep Cut and Cigar Box Battles. Other gamers use polystyrene or MDF baseboards that can be bought or carved into realistic terrain surfaces. The terrain is best placed on top of the mat, and for our region, you will need plenty of hills, rivers, gullies, and a few trees. Rough trench systems and stakes were a feature of Ottoman defensive positions on the battlefield. Eastern European buildings are available from several firms, including Grand Manner, Warbases, Sarissa, and Hovels. Most terrain features can be modelled from scratch with basic modelling skills, and there are plenty of online resources.

Scenarios

Wargame scenarios are a good way to get started with wargaming the typical actions of the period. We have included a couple of introductory scenarios here. However, more will be available on the author's website (www.balkanhistory.org).

Battle of Khotyn

This game is based on the first significant battle of the Russo-Ottoman War, 1768–74. The town and fortress of Khotyn was on the Dniester River near the Polish border, where the Russians had been fighting the Polish Confederates in the War of the Bar Confederation. It was one of a string of Ottoman forts defending the river line.

The Russian First Army, under the command of Prince Golitsyn, was tasked with capturing Khotyn. His army had around 40,000 effectives, and the Ottoman garrison was around 20,000 strong, commanded by Hussein Pasha. Nearby detachments of around 50,000 men could support him, and the 80,000-strong Tatar army was down the river at Bender. The main Ottoman field army commanded by the grand vizier was moving slowly towards the theatre of war.

Battle of Khotyn (Carronade 2025)

The battle had three phases. The Ottomans had built a trench line in front of the fortress, which, after defeating a sortie from the garrison, was captured by the Russians. However, the suburbs were set on fire, halting the planned storming. As the Russians had no siege guns and were running low on supplies, they retreated across the river. Golitsyn tried again, this time crossing the river north of Khotyn. He formed his army into a large square and fought off repeated Ottoman cavalry attacks. However, after reaching the fortress, he ran short of supplies again and withdrew over the river. Catherine replaced Golitsyn with Rumyantsev, but the Ottomans built a bridge over the river before he could arrive and attacked the Russian camp. A cavalry attack was defeated, but the Janissaries and other infantry pushed back the Russians before a flank attack from a detachment in the woods threw them back to Khotyn. The Ottoman bridge collapsed in heavy rain, and the grand vizier, with his army demoralised and short of food, abandoned the fortress on 7 September.

Scenario

At the Carronade 2025 wargames show in Falkirk, Glasgow and District Wargaming Society (GDWS) presented a compact representation of the final battle in 28mm. The rules were Dan Mersey's *Rebels and Patriots*. The Ottomans were crossing the bridge, and a Russian force was sent to stop them. The army lists are set out below.

Russian

Unit	Type	Upgrade	Size	Speed	Fight	Disc	Firing/Range	Pts	Specials
Line Infantry	Line Infantry		12	6	6	0	5+/18"	4	First Fire/fight, Close order
Line Infantry	Line Infantry		12	6	6	0	5+/18"	4	First Fire/fight, Close order
Line Infantry	Line Infantry		12	6	6	0	5+/18"	4	First Fire/fight, Close order
Line Infantry	Line Infantry		12	6	6	0	5+/18"	4	First Fire/fight, Close order
Line Infantry	Line Infantry		12	6	6	0	5+/18"	4	First Fire/fight, Close order
Cossack foot	Skirmishers		6	8	6	0	5+/12"	4	Evade, skirmish, fight 1/2 dice, ignore terrain, cover
Cossack Horse	Light Cavalry	Poor shot	6	12	6	0	6+/12"	3	Evade/Counter, Skirmish
Cossack Horse	Light Cavalry	Poor shot	6	12	6	0	6+/12"	3	Evade/Counter, Skirmish
Cuirassiers	Shock Cavalry	Small	6	10	5	0		6	Counter, follow up, close order
Carabiniers	Light Cavalry	Aggressive	6	12	5	0	5+/12"	4	Counter, Skirmish, NOT fire action,
Artillery	Light art		4	4'	6	0	5+/24	4	Hard cover to cover, arc, +1 close order, cover
							Total	44	

Ottoman

Unit	Type	Upgrade	Size	Speed	Fight	Disc	Firing/Range	Pts	Specials
Jannisaries	Line Infantry	Aggressive, Poor Shot	12	6	5+	0	6+/18"	4	First Fire/flight
Jannisaries	Line Infantry	Aggressive, Poor Shot	12	6	5+	0	6+/18"	4	First Fire/flight
Jannisaries	Line Infantry	Aggressive, Poor Shot	12	6	5+	0	6+/18"	4	First Fire/flight
Jannisaries	Line Infantry	Aggressive, Poor Shot	12	6	5+	0	6+/18"	4	First Fire/flight
Sekhans	Skirmishers	Good shot	6	8	6+	0	4+/12"	4	evade, skirmish, fight 1/2 dice, ignore terrain, cover
Levend	Line Infantry	Green, Poor shot	12	6	6+	-1	6+/18"	2	First Fire/flight
Levend	Line Infantry	Green, Poor shot	12	6	6+	-1	6+/18"	2	First Fire/flight
Sipahis	Light Cavalry		6	12	6+	0	5+/12"	4	Evade/Counter, Skirmish, No fire action
Sipahis	Light Cavalry		6	12	6+	0	5+/12"	4	Evade/Counter, Skirmish, No fire action
Sipahis	Light Cavalry	Green	6	12	6	-1	5+/12"	3	Evade/Counter, Skirmish, No fire action,
Tatars	Light Cavalry	Green, Good shot	6	12	6+	-1	4+/12"	5	Evade/Counter, Skirmish, No fire action
Tatars	Light Cavalry	Green,	6	12	6+	-1	5+/12"	4	Evade/Counter, Skirmish, No fire action
								44	

Battle of Rymnik (Coming, Suvorov!)

The Battle of Rymnik was fought on 22 September 1789, in Wallachia, near Râmnicu Sărat (now in Romania) during the Russo-Ottoman War of 1787–1792 and the Austro-Ottoman War of 1788–1791.

After their defeat at the Battle of Focșani (31 July 1789), Grand Vizier Cenaze Hasan Pasha reinforced the main field army to a strength of around 100,000 men, including 40,000 Janissaries, 40,000 cavalry, and 20,000 other infantry, supported by 85 guns. He started the new offensive with a night march from Braila to attack Coburg's 18,000-strong Austrian army on the Râmnicul Sărat River in Wallachia, south of Focșani. Coburg managed to fight off the initial attack from the Ottoman vanguard on 19 September and called on Suvorov's 7,000-strong division for support. Suvoruv replied simply, "Coming, Suvorov!" and quickly marched to their aid, covering about 97 kilometres in two and a half days, arriving on 21 September. The Ottomans had camped in the river basin of the Rymna (Râmna) and Rymnik Rivers, fortifying three camps six kilometres apart. Despite being outnumbered four to one, Suvorov proposed attacking and defeating the larger Ottoman army piecemeal.

Battle of Rymnik (Claymore 2025)

Scenario

On the evening of 21 September, Russian engineers discovered a crossing point on the Rymna, and Suvorov led his column across the river, forming six squares. They advanced six kilometres south towards the Ottoman camp at Tyrgo Kukuli. After an artillery exchange, some 12,000 Ottoman troops surged out of a gully to attack the Russian left flank. The square was breached in several places, but by deploying reserves and fire support from the neighbouring squares, the Ottomans retreated, and Suvorov moved his division to the left to support Coburg.

The game was played at the Claymore 2025 wargames show in Edinburgh using 28mm figures from various ranges. The rules were *Lust for Glory*, a variant of the popular *To the Strongest* and *For King and Parliament* rules by Simon Miller, which GDWS are playtesting for the author. The scenario begins with the Russians having crossed the river and facing an Ottoman attack. The Russian aim is to capture the Ottoman camp and destroy the army.

Russian 1789

Unit	Size	Weapons	Quality	Drill	Save	Hits	Victory	Dash	Melee	Cost	Comment
Commanding General					2+					6	
Grenadiers	Standard	Inf. Fl. Sb. Bg	Superior	Well drilled	6+	3	3		3	14	
Infantry battalion	Standard	Inf. Fl. Sb. Bg	Ordinary	Drilled	7+	3	3		3	11	
Infantry battalion	Standard	Inf. Fl. Sb. Bg	Ordinary	Drilled	7+	3	3		3	11	
Infantry battalion	Standard	Inf. Fl. Sb. Bg	Ordinary	Drilled	7+	3	3		3	11	
Infantry battalion	Standard	Inf. Fl. Sb. Bg	Ordinary	Drilled	7+	3	3		3	11	
Infantry battalion	Standard	Inf. Fl. Sb. Bg	Ordinary	Drilled	7+	3	3		3	11	
Field Artillery		Art. F. New			7+	1	1		1	5	
Field Artillery		Art. F. New			7+	1	1		1	5	
Major General					2+					6	
Carabiniers	Standard	Horse Ch.	Ordinary	Drilled	7+	2	2	2	2	10	
Hussars	Standard	Horse Sh.	Ordinary	Drilled	7+	2	2	1	2	8	Poor mount
Major-General					2+					6	
Cuirassiers	Standard	Horse Ch.	Superior	Drilled	6+	2	2	2	2	12	
Carabiniers	Standard	Horse Ch.	Ordinary	Drilled	7+	2	2	2	2	10	
Cossacks	Standard	Horse Sh.	Ordinary	Drilled	7+	2	2	1	2	8	Poor mount
Total										**145**	

Ottoman 1789

Unit	Size	Weapons	Quality	Drill	Save	Hits	Victory	Dash	Melee	Cost	Comment
Commanding General					2+					6	
Janissaries	Standard	Inf, Fl	Superior	Drilled	6+	3	3		3	14	Shock
Janissaries	Standard	Inf, Fl	Superior	Drilled	6+	3	3		3	14	Shock
Janissaries	Standard	Inf, Fl	Superior	Drilled	6+	3	3		3	14	Shock
Militia	Standard	Inf. Fl.	Ordinary	Poor drill	7+	3	3		1	9	
Field Artillery		Art. F.			7+	1	1		1	4	
Pasha					2+					6	
Sipahi of the Porte	Standard	Horse, Ch. Cu.	Superior	Drilled	6+	2	2	2	1	14	
Sipahi	Standard	Horse, Ch.	Ordinary		7+	2	2	2	2	10	
Sipahi	Standard	Horse, Ch.	Ordinary		7+	2	2	2	2	10	
Bosnian Horse	Standard	Horse, Ch.	Ordinary		7+	2	2	2	2	10	
Pasha					2+					6	
Sipahi	Standard	Horse, Ch.	Ordinary		7+	2	2	2	2	10	
Sipahi	Standard	Horse, Ch.	Ordinary		7+	2	2	2	2	10	
Sipahi	Standard	Horse, Ch.	Ordinary		7+	2	2	2	2	10	
Bosnian Horse	Standard	Horse, Ch.	Ordinary		7+	2	2	2	2	10	
Total										**151**	

Storming of Berezan Island

This is a small skirmish scenario covering the assault on Berezan Island by Black Sea Cossacks in November 1788. Berezan Island is situated in the Black Sea at the entrance of the Dnieper-Bug Estuary, in modern-day Ukraine. It is some eight kilometres from the Ottoman fortress of Ochakov, which was being besieged by Russian forces. The island measures approximately 900 metres in length and 320 metres in width, and commands the entrance to the river. It had previously been a Greek and Varangian colony. Its position made it a strategic target for the Russians prior to the storming of Ochakov, planned for the following month. The Russians had captured Kinburn on the other side of the estuary at the start of the war, which would make a larger amphibious scenario, if you want one.

Janissaries

The Ottomans had garrisoned the island with approximately 300 troops, commanded by Osman Pasha, in what the Russians referred to as the Berezanskaya fortress. The diagram submitted in the Russian report shows a wall with two bastions on the two seaward sides. The landward side has a ditch and embankment. The Cossack force consisted of around 600 men in small Cossack boats, commanded by Colonel Chepegoyu. They landed on the northern side of the island, supported by guns from their boats and frigates, under fire from Ottoman batteries. They stormed the fortress, capturing it with fewer than 30 casualties.[1] This game is best suited for skirmish rules, and we used the *Rebels and Patriots* rules. The game covers a Russian assault on one part of the defences. The Russian objective is to capture the wall.

Ottoman Garrison

1 unit of 12 Janissaries: line infantry, aggressive. 5 pts.
3 units of 12 Levend: line infantry, green. 9 pts.
1 medium gun: 6 pts.

Russians

1 unit of 12 veteran Cossacks: natives, veteran, aggressive, poor shots. 6 pts.
3 units of 12 Cossacks: natives, poor shots. 9 pts.
2 medium guns (naval guns): 12 pts.

Ottoman and Russian cavalry

---

1. Sapozhnikov, I., *Island Berezan: 17 November 1788* (Ilyichevsk, Gratek, 2000).

Chapter Fifteen

Bibliography

Anonymous, *An Authentic Narrative of the Russian Expedition Against the Turks by Sea and Land* (London, 1772)
Alexander, J, *Catherine the Great: Life and Legend* (Oxford, 1989)
Anderson, R, *Naval Wars in the Levant 1559–1853* (Liverpool University, 1952)
Anscombe, F, *The Ottoman Balkans, 1750–1830* (Princeton, 2006)
Agoston, G, in Jeremy Black ed., *European Warfare, 1453–1815* (Macmillan, 1999), *Ottoman Warfare in Europe 1453–1826*, pp. 118-144.
Aksan, V, *Ottoman Wars 1700–1870* (Pearson, 2007)
Aksan, V, *Whatever Happened to the Janissaries? Mobilization for the 1768–1774 Russo-Ottoman War* (War in History, Vol. 5, No. 1, January 1998)
Aksan, V, *Mutiny and the Eighteenth Century Ottoman Army* (Turkish Studies Association Bulletin, Vol. 22, No. 1, Spring 1998)
Aksan, V, *An Ottoman Statesman in War and Peace* (Brill, 1995)
Baddeley, J, *The Russian Conquest of the Caucasus* (Longmans, 1908)
Black, J, *European Warfare 1660–1815* (UCL, 1994)
Blease, B, *Suvorof* (Constable, 1920)
Bostan, H, *Defending the Ottoman Capital Against the Russian Threat: Late Eighteenth Century Fortifications of Istanbul* (Istanbul Sehir University, 2020)
Bulatov, A, C Delano Smith, and F Herbert, *Andrew Dury's Map of the Present Seat of War Between the Russian, Poles and Turks, 1769* (Imago Mundi, Vol. 53, 2001)
Cunningham, A, *Anglo-Ottoman Encounters in the Age of Revolution* (Frank Cass, 1993)
Chaffetz, D, *Raiders, Rulers, and Traders: The Horse and the Rise of Empires* (Norton, 2024)
Cross, A, (Ed.), *An English Lady at the Court of Catherine the Great* (Crest, 1989)
Cruse, M, and H Hoogenboom, (Trans.), *The Memoirs of Catherine the Great* (Random House, 2006)
Davies, B, *The Russo-Turkish War, 1768–1774* (Bloomsbury, 2016)

De Waal, T, *The Caucasus* (Oxford, 2010)
Dixon, S, *The Modernisation of Russia* (Cambridge, 2012)
Duffy, C, *Russia's Military Way to the West* (Routledge, 1981)
Duffy, C, *Instrument of War: The Austrian Army in the Seven Years War*, (Helion, 2020)
Duffy, C, *The Army of Maria Theresa* (Terence Wise, 1990)
Duffy, C, *The Military Experience in the Age of Reason* (Routledge, 1987)
Erickson, C, *Great Catherine* (Simon & Schuster, 1994)
Golder, F, *John Paul Jones in Russia* (Doubleday, 1927)
Goodwin, G, *The Janissaries* (Saqi Books, 1994)
Gundogdu, B, *Ottoman Constructions of the Morea Rebellion, 1770s* (University of Toronto, 2012)
Fedosov, D, *Diary of General Patrick Gordon of Auchleuchries 1635–1699* (6 volumes) (Aberdeen University Press, 2010)
Fisher, A, *The Russian Annexation of the Crimea* (Cambridge, 1970)
Flaherty, C, *The Napoleonic Ottoman Army* (Partizan Press, 2019)
Hanioglu, S, *A Brief History of the Late Ottoman Empire* (Princeton, 2008)
Hartley, J, *The Volga: A History of Russia's Greatest River* (Yale, 2021)
Hickok, M, *Ottoman Military Administration in Eighteenth-Century Bosnia* (Brill, 1997)
Hochedlinger, M, *Austria's Wars of Emergence, 1683–1797* (Longman, 2003)
Itzkowitz, N, *Ottoman Empire and Islamic Tradition* (Chicago, 1972)
Jelavich, B, *History of the Balkans* (Cambridge, 1983)
Kahn, A, and K Rubin-Detlev, (Trans.), *Catherine the Great: Selected Letters* (Oxford, 2018)
Kagan, F, and R Higham, (Ed.), *The Military History of Tsarist Russia* (Palgrave, 2002)
Kaplan, H, *Russia and the Outbreak of the Seven Years' War* (California, 1968)
Kaplan, H, *The First Partition of Poland* (Columbia University Press, 1962)
Karkocha, M, *The Russo-Turkish war (the campaign of 1789) in the light of reports from "Pamiętnik Historyczno-Polityczno-Ekonomiczny"* (Review of Historical Sciences, Vol. XVI, 3, 2017).
Kauko, R, *Suvorov: Generalissimus-Genius* (Helsinki, SHS, 1989)
Khodarkovsky, M, *Russia's Steppe Frontier* (Indiana Press, 2004)
Kolodziejczyk, D, *The Crimean Khanate and Poland-Lithuania* (Brill, 2011)
Konstam, A, *Russian Army of the Seven Years War*, 2 volumes (Osprey, 1996)
Laverne, L de, *The Life of Field Marshal Souvarof* (Baltimore, 1814)
Levy, A, *Military Reform and the Problem of Centralization in the Ottoman Empire in the Eighteenth Century* (Middle Eastern Studies Vol. 18, No. 3, July 1982), pp. 227–249.

Lohr, E, and M Poe, (Ed.), *The Military and Society in Russia 1450–1917* (Brill, 2002)
Lieven, D, *The Cambridge History of Russia*, Vol. 2 (Cambridge, 2006)
Marriot, J, *Anglo-Russian Relations 1689–1943* (Methuen, 1944)
Massie, R, *Catherine the Great: Portrait of a Woman* (Head of Zeus, 2012)
Mayer, M, *Joseph II and the Austro-Ottoman War, 1788–1791* (University of Cambridge Repository, 2002)
McNeill, W, *Europe's Steppe Frontier, 1500–1800* (Chicago, 1964)
Mikaberidze, A, *Kutuzov: A Life in War and Peace* (Oxford, 2022)
Montefiore, S, *Prince of Princes: The Life of Potemkin* (Phoenix Press, 2000)
Muller, K, *Der Vorstoβ der russischen Flotte in den Griechischen Archipel, 1769 bis 1775* (Redaktionsbüro OSTPROJEKT, 2013)
Mugnai, B, *The Ottoman Army of the Napoleonic Wars* (Helion, 2022)
Nicolle, D, *Armies of the Ottoman Turks 1300–1774* (Osprey, 1983)Nicolle, D, *Armies of the Ottoman Empire 1775–1820* (Osprey, 1998)
Ostapchuk, V, and S Bilyayeva, *The Ottoman Northern Black Sea Frontier at Akkerman Fortress* (Proceedings of the British Academy, 156, 2009), pp. 137–170.
Özer, A, *The Ottoman-Russian Relations Between the Years 1774–1787* (Bilkent University, 2008)
Panaite, V, *Ottoman Law of War and Peace: The Ottoman Empire and its Tributaries from the North of the Danube* (Brill, 2019)
Resmi, A, *A Chronicle of the 1768–1774 Russian-Ottoman War*, (Isis Press, 2011)
Sapozhnikov, I, *Island Berezan: 17 November 1788* (Ilyichevsk, Gratek, 2000)
Schroeder, P, *The Transformation of European Politics 1763–1848* (Oxford, 1994)
Shaw, S, *History of the Ottoman Empire and Modern Turkey*, Volume 1 (Cambridge, 1976)
Shirokorad, A, *Admirals and Corsairs of Catherine the Great* (Moscow, Beye, 2006)
Smith, J, (Ed.), *Beyond the Limits: The Concept of Space in Russian History and Culture* (SHS/Helsinki, 1999)
Steuart, F, *Scottish Influences in Russian History* (Maclehose, 1913)
Stoyanov, A, *Russia marches South: army reform and battlefield performance in Russia's Southern campaigns, 1695–1739* (Universiteit Leiden, 2017)
Sugar, P, *Southeastern Europe under Ottoman Rule, 1354–1804* (Washington, 1977)
Tott, F de, *Memoirs of Baron de Tott* (G & J Robinson, London, 1785)
Uyar, M, and E Erickson, *A Military History of the Ottomans: From Osman to Atatürk* (Praeger, 2009)
Velikanov, V, *Ottoman Army's Strength and Organization at the beginning of the Russo-Turkish War of 1768–1774* (Academic Publishing House, 2018)
Viskovatov, A, *Uniforms of the Russian Army in the XVIII Century – Volume 1*

(Soldiershop, 2017)
Ward, L, *The Empress and the English Doctor* (One World, 2022)
Wieczynski, J, *The Russian Frontier* (University of Virginia, 1976)
Yener, E, *Ottoman Seapower and Naval Technology during Catherine II's Turkish Wars 1768–92* (International Naval Journal, Vol. 9, Issue 1, 2016)
Yener, E, *Reconsidering the Campaign of Dnieper Liman* (Vestnik of Saint Petersburg University. History, 2022, vol. 67, issue 3), pp. 817–832.
Zorin, A, *By Fables Alone* (Academic Studies Press, 2014)

Chapter Sixteen

About the Author

D ave Watson was born in Liverpool and has lived in Scotland for thirty-five years. He lives with his wife, Liz, in Ayrshire.

He is the author of *Cyprus 1974* (BMH 2024), *HMS Ambuscade: 1746 to the Present Day* (CHT 2024), *The Frontier Sea: The Napoleonic Wars in the Adriatic* (BMH, 2023), *Chasing the Soft Underbelly: Turkey and the Second World War* (Helion, 2023), *Ripped Apart, Cyprus Crisis, 1963–1974* (Helion, 2023). He is a contributing author to several current affairs books and publications.

Dave is the editor of *Balkan Military History* (www.balkanhistory.org), which has covered the military history of the Balkans for over twenty-seven years. He has also contributed to several magazines, journals, and online publications. His publications can be found on the website and his blog (balkandave.blogspot.com).

He is a graduate in Scots Law from the University of Strathclyde, a Fellow of the Royal Society of Arts, and an Associate Fellow of the Royal Historical Society. He retired in 2018 from his post as Head of Policy and Public Affairs at UNISON Scotland and now works part time as a policy consultant and director of the Scottish think tank The Jimmy Reid Foundation. He is the secretary of Glasgow and District Wargaming Society, one of the UK's longest-running wargame clubs.

The author acknowledges the assistance of members and other wargamers in Scotland in playtesting the scenarios in this book. He also thanks friends in Türkiye, Romania, and Moldova for their hospitality during his visits to the region, as well as those staffing the museums and historical sites in the region. He is also grateful to the staff at the National Archives (Kew), the British Library, and the National Library of Scotland for their assistance, as well as to the scholars who have researched this conflict. Any errors or omissions are the author's alone. And finally, he thanks his long-suffering wife, for her support on the trips and the time it takes to research and write his books.

You can follow Dave on X (formerly Twitter) at @Balkan_Dave. Or BlueSky @balkandave.bsky.social

www.ingramcontent.com/pod-product-compliance
Lightning Source LLC
Chambersburg PA
CBHW071206070526
44584CB00019B/2937